36

$4.50
Tax .29
$4.79

Texas

AN ILLUSTRATED HISTORY

Texas

An Illustrated History

David G. McComb

Oxford University Press

New York • Oxford

For Mary Alice

Oxford University Press

Oxford New York
Athens Auckland Bangkok Bombay
Calcutta Cape Town Dar es Salaam Delhi
Florence Hong Kong Istanbul Karachi
Kuala Lumpur Madras Madrid Melbourne
Mexico City Nairobi Paris Singapore
Taipei Tokyo Toronto
and associated companies in

Berlin Ibadan

Copyright © 1995 by David G. McComb
Published by Oxford University Press, Inc.,
200 Madison Avenue, New York, New York 10016

Oxford is a registered trademark of Oxford University Press

Design: Sandy Kaufman
Layout: Loraine Machlin
Picture research: Wendy P. Wills

Library of Congress Cataloging-in-Publication Data
Texas, an illustrated history / David G. McComb
        p.   cm.
Includes bibliographical references and index.
1. Texas—History—Juvenile literature. [1. Texas—History.]
I. Title.
F386.3.M37   1995
976.4—dc20   94-23279
                CIP

ISBN 0-19-509246-5 (trade ed.)
ISBN 0-19-509247-3 (library ed.)

9 8 7 6 5 4 3 2 1

Printed in Hong Kong
on acid-free paper

On the cover: Circular Cowboy, by Mary Anita Bonner, circa 1929.

Frontispiece: Cowboys from the XIT ranch in the Texas Panhandle gather around the chuck wagon for a meal.

Title page: West Side Main Plaza, San Antonio, Texas, by W.G.M. Samuel, 1849.

Contents page: A $50 bill printed by the Republic of Texas in 1840.

Contents

*Artist Jean Louis Theodore
Gentilz painted the original
version of this romanticized
view of a nomadic Indian
tribe's camp in 1844. However, this version of the
painting dates from 1896,
long after the last Native
Americans had left Texas.*

Chapter One
The Native Americans and the Land

L ate in 1982 archaeologist Wayne Young discovered three severed finger bones protruding from the soil at a highway construction site near the small town of Leander in central Texas. Since 1970 the Texas government had required the highway department to investigate historical places before the construction of roads could begin. This time highway workers had sliced open an ancient Indian burial ground. Inches away from the fingers, Young discovered the skull and skeleton of a woman who had been about five feet three inches in height and who had died when she was around 30 years old. She was buried lying on her right side, with her head resting on her hands and her legs drawn up near her chest. In the pit with the skeleton were a grinding stone and a fossil shark's tooth that may have been part of a necklace.

Leann, as the archaeologists named the skeleton, was 9,000 to 10,000 years old. She was a Paleo-Indian, a member of the earliest human group in what is now Texas. Her forebears, who were much like modern human beings in physical characteristics, had migrated across the Bering Strait in

Alaska, drifted southward, and eventually pursued prehistoric bison for food on the lush prairies of the Texas plains. At the town of Plainview in West Texas archaeologists have studied a long, narrow site where 100 ancient buffalo skeletons were piled up with bones a foot deep mixed together with flint tools and projectile points. It is thought that Paleo-Indians surrounded a herd and slaughtered it, or perhaps scared the bison into a gully, where they killed the animals within a short time.

Blowing sand near Midland exposed bits of another Paleo-Indian skeleton in 1953, and in 1970 the fossilized bones of a 30- to 40-year-old man and a 12-year-old child were found beneath a rock ledge near Waco. The man and child had been buried much like Leann, but they lay on their left sides, with their heads resting on turtle shells. With them the archaeologists found seashell beads probably from the Gulf Coast, a bone needle, and stone tools most likely from the prehistoric Alibates Flint Quarries of West Texas. Much is still unknown about these early Texans, but the artifacts indicate an interest in trade, the use of a notable prehistoric source of flint, and

a reverence, or concern, for people who had died.

Archaic-age (5000 B.C. to A.D. 700) Indians followed the Paleo-Indians in Texas. During this time the Indians developed a greater variety of stone tools, such as axes, picks, drills, and dart points. Like other peoples around the world, they invented a bow and arrow for hunting, acquired dogs as traveling companions, and ate more plants than their predecessors. Modern Native Americans in Texas evolved from these Archaic-age Indians and improved their lives even more through the use of agriculture.

By the time Europeans came to the New World in 1492 the Indians had divided into tribes with different cultures, or patterns of living. The Jumano Indians lived in permanent houses made of adobe, a sun-dried brick made of mud and straw. They settled along the Rio Grande and Rio Concho, made pots, planted crops of corn, and hunted buffalo. Drought had weakened the tribe by the time the Spanish arrived in the 16th century and the Jumanos were eating their seed corn in order to stay alive. This meant that they had no seeds to plant in the future. After fighting with the Spanish and their old enemy the Apache Indians, the

Jumanos, having lost population, disappeared by the late 18th century.

Across Texas in the eastern pine forests lived another tribe noted for its agriculture. The Caddo Indians were probably the best farmers in North America. They grew crops of corn, melons, squash, beans, sunflowers, and tobacco. They cleared a field first by setting it on fire, and then stirring the soil with sticks and planting the seeds. From year to year they saved seeds to plant the next spring. In addition, they ate deer, buffalo, bears, ducks, rabbits, snakes, fish, and mice. The Caddos lived in large round huts made of poles covered with straw, and made clay pots, straw baskets, and musical flutes of bird bones. Both men and women worked at farming, and women were treated with greater respect than in other tribes. The Caddos called themselves Taychas, meaning "friends." When the Spanish heard this, they used the word to mean friendly Indians. From this term comes the word *Texas,* the name of the state.

To the west of the Caddos lived the Wichita tribes. They had been pushed southward into Texas during fights with the Osage Indians of Kansas. They were much like the Caddos and spoke a similar language. Their culture, however, placed a greater burden of work on women. An 18th-century French soldier and diplomat, Athanase de Mezières, observed: "The women tan, sew, and paint the skins, fence the fields, care for the cornfields, harvest the crops, cut and fetch the firewood, prepare the food, build the houses, and rear the children, their constant care stopping at nothing that contributes to the comfort and pleasure of their husbands. The latter devote themselves wholly to the chase and to warfare."

Most North American Indians painted and tattooed their bodies. The Wichitas, apparently fond of decoration, were extreme in the extent of their tattoos. The marking was done by scratching the skin until it bled and rubbing charcoal dust into the wound. The men traced lines from the outside edges of their eyes and downward from the corners of their mouths. They drew eagle claws on the backs of their hands and marked their arms and chests with symbols of victory in war. The women tattooed lines down the tops of their noses and around their mouths and chins. They placed zigzag lines on their arms and circles around their breasts as marks of beauty.

An archaeologist at work at a site near Midland in October 1953. Found at the site were several pieces of fossilized skull, roughly 10,000 years old, belonging to a woman archaeologists named Midland Minnie.

Alfred Jacob Miller painted these Indians hunting a buffalo in 1837. The buffalo were not only the Indians' main source of food but also provided them with clothing and shelter. The horses, brought to the New World by the Spanish, gave the Indians increased mobility and made hunting more efficient.

To the west of the Wichitas, on the Great Plains, lived the Comanche and Apache tribes. The Comanches became the main Indian enemy of the Spanish and American settlers and are the tribe most Texans think about when they hear the word *Indian*. They were nomads, always moving and searching for food. Originally, they came out of the Rocky Mountains in what is now southern Colorado, traveling on foot and following the Arkansas River valley. Early in the 18th century they acquired horses by theft and trade from the Spanish in New Mexico. They soon became expert horse people whose children began to ride almost as soon as they could walk. Warriors learned to fight and hunt on horseback and became the best light cavalry (unarmored soldiers on horses) in the history of the world. By 1750 they controlled the southern plains from what is now Colorado and Kansas into West Texas. This area was called the Comancheria.

Buffalo was the Comanches' main food, but they also hunted bears, antelope, and longhorn cattle. Along the trail they would pick wild plums, grapes, mulberries, persimmons, pecans, and tubers (edible roots). They learned to make pemmican, a trail mix of dried buffalo meat mixed with nuts, berries, and buffalo fat. It was carried in a pouch made from the intestine of a buffalo. They often ate their meat raw—the fresh liver of a downed buffalo, for instance—and when they were starving they would eat almost anything—including their horses. They grew nothing and bartered for corn and tobacco.

The Comanches lived in portable, cone-shaped tepees made of long poles and buffalo hides. For protection from the weather the entry flap at the bottom as well as the vent at the top faced away from the wind. Inside was a fireplace or loose stones for cooking and warmth, and animal skins for beds. The Comanche tepee was supposedly more comfortable than the log cabins of white pioneers.

Comanche men fought and hunted with spears and short bows and arrows. At first

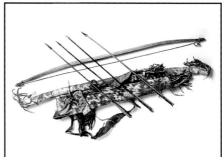

The bows Comanche men used were made of hickory and strung with buffalo sinews. Arrows were made of dogwood and tipped at first with stone, but later with iron or steel. Their shields were made of bison hide and decorated with feathers and horse tails.

the weapons were tipped with sharp stone, and later with iron or steel acquired from Europeans. They carried painted bison-hide shields that could deflect enemy arrows and sometimes a glancing bullet. The rim of the shield was decorated with feathers, scalps, and horse tails. From a galloping horse a Comanche man could drive an arrow all the way through a running buffalo.

Meeting in council, the men made the decisions for the tribe, but any warrior could lead a raiding group. They often struck in small bands by the light of a full moon to steal and kill. They divided their loot quickly and, if chased, they would split apart, each warrior fleeing alone. This made them difficult to catch. They particularly liked to steal horses, but after the Civil War they stole cattle to sell in New Mexico. This brought them into ongoing conflict with ranchers and the state.

War was a necessary part of their lives and boys were trained to become fighters. Stealing horses, scalping an enemy, and

touching a live opponent were considered the bravest of acts. Such accomplishments were "coups," and warriors would "count coup" at tribal gatherings. It was a type of bragging that was a part of Comanche culture.

Not even the fierce Apache Indians could stand against the Comanches. The Apache tribes were forced out of West Texas into New Mexico and to the south. The Kiowa Apaches eventually formed an alliance with the Comanches, while the Lipan Apaches were crushed between the Comanches in the north and the Spanish in the south. In the later 18th century the Lipans were squeezed into desert land, where poverty eventually reduced them to beggars. At the same time, the Jicarilla Apaches moved to New Mexico to live with the Pueblo Indians. It was renegade Apaches, however, who fought the last Texas Indian war, a conflict that lingered from 1879 until 1881.

Native American tribes to the south of Comancheria and along the Gulf Coast were the most primitive of the Texas Indians. They all hunted, fished, and gathered wild edible foods, but none of them planted anything. The Tonkawas ate almost everything, including rats and skunks, and practiced ritual cannibalism, which meant that they ate parts of human beings for religious reasons. John H. Jenkins, a soldier and writer of the 19th century, observed Tonkawas yelling and dancing while they ate the boiled hands and feet of a Wichita warrior. They thought that such action gave them the spirit power of the dead man. Settlers at the time, however, thought that the Tonkawas were cannibals.

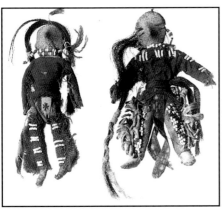

A drum and a pair of dolls from the Tonkawa Indians. Drums were used by the Tonkawas in their "scalp dances," in which the warriors would move rhythmically and eat pieces of a dead enemy.

The Karankawa Indians had a culture similar to that of the Tonkawas. They roamed the coast in small bands almost naked looking for food. They were often hungry and ate oysters, clams, turtles, fish, berries, deer, bears, and tubers from underwater plants. They shoved crude dugout canoes with poles, used nets to catch fish, and smeared their bodies with smelly alligator fat to repel mosquitoes. The Karankawas were the first Texas Indians to meet Europeans, in 1528, and they saved the lives of the shipwrecked Spaniards on their shore. Hard experiences, however, soon turned them against the newcomers.

The Karankawas were among the first Texas Indians to be killed off. There were fights with Europeans, and the Indians suffered from diseases brought by white people. As their population thinned, they drifted into Mexico and became extinct in the 1850s. As naturalist Roy Bedichek wrote in 1950 with sympathy, admiration, and irony, "The Karankawas are gone. Only bitter memories of them remain. In the minds of our people they are eternally damned, largely because they refused a culture we offered, resisting our proffered blessings to the last."

So it might be said for all Texas Indians. They resisted the culture brought by the European and American invaders. Only two small reservations now exist for Indians in Texas, and they are for tribes that came later: the Alabama-Coushattas in the east and the Tiguas in the west.

The Native Americans in Texas faced united and determined opponents, who in the long run overwhelmed them. The Indians lost because of infectious European diseases, slaughter of the buffalo, and the larger numbers and better technology of the newcomers. It was not just firearms that defeated them, but also better methods of farming, communications, and transportation. The Indians lost to a stronger enemy, just as earlier Texas tribes had lost to the Comanches. The Native Americans were caught in a flood of settlers that carried the Spanish and American cultures from the Atlantic to the Pacific coasts. The Indians, nevertheless, were the first to experience the land of Texas and to utilize its resources. It was a vast land, and almost everyone today is impressed not only with its size but with how different Texas is from other states. Until Alaska became a state in 1959, Texas was the largest in the United States. Now it is second largest and measures about 770 miles from east to west and 800 miles from north to south, a total of 267,000 square miles. It takes a day and a half to cross the state by automobile. There is plenty of room for changes in appearance and the Texas Department of Highways calls the state the "Land of Contrasts."

The reason for these contrasts is the changing topography, the variety of landforms across the state. In the United States there exist eight main types of landforms. Most states embrace only one, but Texas has four of them—Rocky Mountains, Great Plains, Interior Lowlands, and Coastal Lowlands. In the Far West the Rocky Mountains enter the state like rocky islands set in beige-colored desert basins. This massive mountain range runs from Alaska through Canada and the United States to Mexico. In Texas the highest point is Guadalupe Peak, 8,751 feet high. But even this seems fairly low

when compared to Mt. McKinley in Alaska, which is over 20,000 feet high.

Elsewhere, the land consists of three gently sloping plains. They are separated by hilly borders called escarpments, where the land drops from one level to the next. The plains formed about 100,000 years ago, when much of Texas was part of a shallow sea. All three slope southeastward toward the Gulf of Mexico. If by magic you could smooth the surface of the land and drop a bowling ball at Dumas, in the Panhandle— the northern part of West Texas that is shaped like the handle of a pan—it would roll into the sea. Then the ball might roll underwater for six more miles on the shallow continental shelf until it dropped off into the deep waters of the Gulf.

It is this slope of the land from an average height of 4,600 feet in West Texas to sea level that causes all the rivers of Texas to flow to the southeast. The major rivers— the Rio Grande, Nueces, San Antonio, Guadalupe, Colorado, Brazos, San Jacinto, Trinity, Sabine, Red, and Canadian—are slow moving, however, and wander over the countryside. The drop in elevation over such a long distance is not great enough to produce the force necessary to turn waterwheels, as rivers in the northeastern United States do. Instead, the brown, sluggish waters form sandbars where silt in the water collects at the bottom of the stream. At times of drought, when there is little rainfall, the streams become shallow and almost dry.

In the early days of Texas settlement only small steamboats risked travel on the rivers, and they often sank after going aground on a sandbar or hitting a broken

tree limb caught in the sand. Such snags could rip holes in the frail wooden hull of a moving steamboat. The streams, however, provided the fresh water necessary for the health of wetlands and for towns located along the banks.

Deep under the land and extending across state boundaries are six major freshwater aquifers. These are vast underground reservoirs formed in sand and porous rock. Over thousands of years, rainwater slowly trickled down into these aquifers. Before this resource of pure water could be used, however, people had to learn to push long pipes into the ground to reach it. Such technology was not used until the latter part of the 19th century.

The rivers begin as small streams in the Great Plains. These high plains, like the Rocky Mountains, reach from Canada through the central United States into Mexico. Before the 20th century this high, dry country was a place to be wary of. Randolph Barnes Marcy, a U.S. Army explorer who marked a trail through this area in 1849, said, "It is an ocean of desert

Indian Rock Art

There are more than 200 sites of Indian pictographs (drawings or paintings) and petroglyphs (carvings) in Texas. They are found on cave walls, cliffs, and rock shelters. Paintings vary from 1 inch to 18 feet in height and are usually red or black. They show human figures, hands and feet, animals, maps, religious symbols, dances, blanket designs, trees, the sun, shields, and masks. At Hueco Tanks, near El Paso, travelers attracted by pools of trapped water have decorated the rocks since the Archaic period.

Near Paint Rock on the Rio Concho there are 1,500 paintings on a limestone cliff that cover a 1,000-year span.

Reasons for the rock art are uncertain. Possibly they were meant to be religious signs, or perhaps they were attempts to record important events. At Hueco Tanks there is a series of white figures indicating a puberty ritual for maidens. At Paint Rock there is a picture of a man wrapped in funeral garments striding upward toward heaven. Perhaps these paintings were simply someone's effort to

show that they were there, just as people today put their initials in wet concrete on city sidewalks. No one knows for certain why the drawings exist or how they were used, but they are reminders of the Native Americans who once moved across the land. Perhaps the Indians, like human beings today, desired to describe their land and life. "We too have lived," the drawings seem to say to modern observers. "We too have thought about life and death, the sun and earth, the animals and the land."

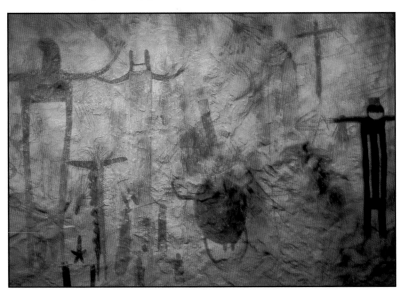

This painting, located on a rock wall in Seminole Canyon State Historical Park, was drawn by an indigenous group who lived there from about 6000 B.C. to A.D. 600. Experts consider this site to have some of the best examples of rock art in the world.

prairie, where the voice of man is seldom heard, and where no living being permanently resides. The almost total absence of water causes all animals to shun it; even the Indians do not venture to cross it except at two or three points, where they find a few small ponds of water."

The southern tip of the Great Plains is called the Edwards Plateau, and the border where the plateau touches the Coastal Plain is called the Balcones Escarpment. The escarpment is known for its choppy little hills and limestone cliffs. The limestone, formed by sediment when Texas was a part of the sea, has seashell fossils embedded in it. This geologic feature of the land is particularly visible where highways have been cut through the hills. Just north of San Antonio are limestone caves. One of them, Inner Space cavern, was discovered by surprised highway engineers in 1963 after their drill bits broke into the hidden underground chamber.

In West Texas, where the Great Plains meet the Interior Lowlands near the towns of Post and Clarendon, there is an abrupt drop in elevation of 300 feet. There the edge of the cap rock, the thick layer of stone that lies under the soil of the High Plains, is visible. On top, the land is as flat as a table; below, rolling eastward, are the gentle hills of the Interior Lowlands. There is greater rainfall in this eastern area, and near Mineral Wells a hardwood forest of oak, elm, hickory, and pecan trees called the Cross Timbers interrupts the undulating prairie land. This was a welcome forest for pioneers who needed wood to build their cabins, warm their homes, and fence their land.

A portion of the Guadalupe Mountains. The highest point in Texas, Guadalupe Peak, is 8,751 feet above sea level.

Running north and south, the Interior Lowlands and the Great Plains both touch the Coastal Lowlands. Along the boundary has grown a line of cities—Del Rio, San Antonio, Waco, Fort Worth, Denton, Denison. Springs of fresh water on this geographic border came from the change in elevation as rainwater from the higher plains bubbled out along the edges. These springs were important in determining the locations of the towns during the time of settlement.

The Coastal Lowlands in Texas are a part of the same landform that goes from Mexico around the Gulf Coast and up the Atlantic shoreline to New York. In Texas the plain is less than 1,000 feet in elevation and gently slips into the Gulf of Mexico. It forms the continental shelf of the Gulf, which extends outward underwater for six miles. The shallow depth of this shelf is one of the main reasons why the waves are smaller on the Gulf Coast than on the Atlantic or Pacific coasts.

The coastal area played a more important role than the mountains or high plains in the history of Texas from 1820 to 1870 because this was the place where pioneers looked for homes. At that time the land was covered with pine forests containing small patches of grassland. The high rainfall and black clay soil were perfect for the growing of cotton. It would not grow on the high, dry plains, and so the western border of the Coastal Plain marked the place where the South met the West. In 1860 to the west of Fort Worth were buffalo, dry grasslands, and Comanche Indians. To the east were cotton fields, slaves, log cabins, and American settlements.

The shoreline of Texas is also important. There, in the bays and wetlands, fresh water from the rivers mixes with the salt water of the Gulf of Mexico to provide a healthful environment for baby shrimp, oysters, birds, snakes, salt grasses, and alligators. Today the Aransas National Wildlife Refuge, between Port Lavaca and Rockport, is the last home for the whooping crane, a water bird threatened with extinction.

Offshore from Galveston to Mexico is a line of barrier islands. They are made of sand carried by rivers into the Gulf and piled up by sea currents. On Galveston Island, the currents scooped out a natural harbor that

The aptly named Red River slowly winds its way across Texas. The Red River has served as a boundary since European exploration and settlement first began. It was the dividing line between Spain and the U.S., between Mexico and the U.S., and between the Republic of Texas and the U.S. Today it serves as the boundary between Texas and Oklahoma and Arkansas.

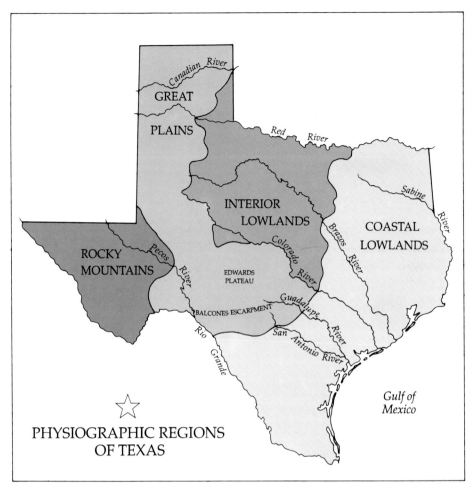

PHYSIOGRAPHIC REGIONS
OF TEXAS

was used as a port at first by pirates and later by merchants. The islands serve as natural barriers to protect the mainland from the destructive pounding of hurricanes driving inland from the Caribbean Sea. People who have chosen to live on the shoreline without paying attention to nature have often suffered.

In contrast to other states, Texas experiences almost all of the weather conditions of the country. Mainly—but not always—Texas weather is mild. Rainfall ranges from 8 inches a year in the extreme west to 58 inches in the extreme east. Generally, ranchers in West Texas expect 20 inches of rain per year; people along the Balcones Escarpment in the central part of the state look for 30 inches. Because of the moisture more people live in the central and eastern parts of the state, but the dry west has a reputation for being a healthful place. "If people want to die," cowboys say in West Texas, "they have to go someplace else."

Snow and sleet are unusual, but there can be blizzards on the Great Plains. In 1956, 33 inches fell in the Panhandle, and in 1985 a relentless cold spell killed the citrus groves of the Rio Grande Valley. Such events are so unusual, however, that in places like Houston schools close when it snows so that the students can have an opportunity to build snowmen. Droughts are also a part of the weather pattern. In 1856, for example, Benno Matthew, a German traveler, was able to cross the nearly dry Colorado River on horseback. Dust storms were a common problem during the 1930s, and in the 1950s the dust was so thick and dark in Dallas that the automatic streetlights turned on at noontime.

Even more frightening are the tornadoes. They form most often in the springtime, when hot air moving from the south meets cold air coming from the north. When the two air fronts meet, they sometimes form tight, whirling storms with inside winds of 500 miles per hour. Destroying whatever they touch, these "twisters" skip across the landscape. South-central Texas is the southern end of a "tornado alley" that points northward like a loaded gun into Iowa. There are about 118 such storms per year, but in 1967 Texas suffered a record 232 tornadoes. People died when tornadoes hit Waco in 1953, Wichita Falls in 1979, and Saragosa in 1987.

The greatest damage, however, has come from hurricanes striking the coastline. These huge swirling storms gather in the mid-Atlantic and move northward through the Gulf of Mexico during the months of June to November. With winds above 75 miles per hour, they hammer the shoreline with high waves, rain, and tornadoes, all part of a hurricane. In 1900 Galveston suffered the worst natural disaster in the history of the United States when a hurricane flooded the island. About 6,000 people died. Hurricane Celia punished Corpus Christi in 1970 with winds measuring 161 miles per hour. Hurricane Alicia hit the Galveston-Houston area in 1983 and popped windows out of downtown skyscrapers. Damage caused by Alicia amounted to $3 billion.

Hurricanes and tornadoes, however, do not strike most Texans. For most people the suffering from weather comes from the cold north winds of winter and the oven-like heat of summer. The "blue norther" is a fast-moving wintertime cold front from the northwest. It appears first as a heavy bank of blue clouds on the horizon. It then arrives with a howl, breaking tree limbs, rattling windows, and causing the temperature to drop as much as 24 degrees in one hour. Pecos Bill, a fictional cowboy invented by journalist Tex O'Reilly, told this story about a norther: Bill rescued a dog running in the cold wind and dragging a 600-pound block of ice stuck to his tail. Bill

broke off the ice and took the dog inside his cabin to warm up. The animal was so cold that when he barked the sound came out frozen. Bill picked up some of the frozen barks and warmed them in a frying pan. The room was soon filled with the noise from the barks—much to the surprise of the dog.

That, of course, is a Texas tall tale. Temperatures, however, do have a wide range in the state. Record high and low temperatures in Abilene, for example, are 110°F and -9°F. Throughout Texas in mid-summer, temperatures are in the 90-degree range. This helps to explain why Texans were the first to build an air-conditioned baseball stadium and why so many people have bought air-conditioning units for their cars, offices, stores, and homes. The prickly summer heat is also the reason for the most famous joke about Texas. In 1855 Philip H. Sheridan, a soldier at Fort Clark, said, "If I owned Hell and Texas, I would rent out Texas and live in Hell!"

This tornado touched down in Austin in 1925. It did not, however, cause damage and death like the "killer" tornadoes that touched down in Goliad (1902), Waco (1953), Lubbock (1970), and Saragosa (1987).

This alligator was photographed at the McFaddin Wildlife Refuge near Port Arthur, which contains one of the densest populations of alligators in Texas.

Texas is home to all four types of poisonous snakes—copperheads, rattlesnakes, coral snakes, and cottonmouth moccasins. The rattlesnake, shown here, is the largest of the four. The longest measured rattlesnake ever found in Texas is 7 feet, 5 inches.

The topography and weather, of course, dictate limits for plants and animals. Pine trees cannot grow on the Great Plains. There is not enough water. Prickly pear cactus plants cannot survive in the coastal wetlands. There is too much water. Only humans can escape these natural limits.

Soil conditions are also important for plants, and there are more than 800 soil mixtures in Texas, a variety uncommon in other states. Early settlers preferred the alluvial dirt found near rivers. This is a mixture of sand, clay, silt, and organic (plant and animal) matter. The parts were mixed by the streams and deposited during floods on nearby land. Pioneers also liked the black, waxy clay of the coastal prairie and joked that the soil was so good that white potatoes planted in this land would turn into sweet potatoes. Another tall tale.

The growing season of favorable temperature and rainfall varies in Texas from 180 days in the Panhandle to 330 days in the Rio Grande Valley. Pioneers planted cotton, corn, wheat, and vegetables for home use. Later, in the 20th century, farmers added rice, grain sorghum, and alfalfa as major crops. During the 1920s, people in the Rio Grande Valley created a citrus business by planting orange and grapefruit trees.

The Indians of East Texas also used agriculture, the technology of growing plants, starting around A.D. 600. They learned to produce corn, squash, beans, tobacco, and sunflowers. The amount of land used for agriculture by the Indians was small and had little effect on the environment. The settlers from Spain and the United States had better tools, such as iron axes and plows, however, and they chopped down trees in order to clear land for planting. The settlers thought of the land as a resource to be used for their own good. The pioneers, consequently, used their tools to change the ecology, or balance of plants and animals on the land.

Early explorers and travelers reported many wild animals, such as wolves, bears, roadrunners, alligators, rabbits, deer, javelinas, ducks, and turkeys. All four types of poisonous snakes live in Texas—copperheads, rattlesnakes, coral snakes, and cottonmouth moccasins. The rare coral snake has the most lethal poison. The largest, however, is the western diamondback rattlesnake, with a head shaped like a triangle and a crisscross pattern of white, brown, and black on its body. The rattle sounds like a handful of small pebbles shaken hard in a tin can. The longest ever measured was 7 feet 5 inches, but Rip Ford, a Texas Ranger of the 19th century, claimed to have seen a 10-foot diamondback in the Cross Timbers. He said that he heard the rattle 100 yards away and that the snake raised its head level to his belt buckle. Ford wisely left the rattlesnake alone.

Buffalo lived on the prairie grasses from the Great Plains to the Coastal Lowland. No mammal, with the exception of human beings, has ever come together in such large numbers. George W. Kendall, a rancher, observed in 1842, "I have stood upon a high roll of the prairies with neither tree nor bush to obstruct the vision in any direction, and seen these animals grazing upon the plain and darkening it at every point." After the Civil War, hunters so diminished the buffalo herds that only a few remained, as pets of ranchers.

Endangered native species, such as this red wolf, are housed at the Texas Zoo in Victoria.

Passenger pigeons, gray and red wolves, bighorn sheep, jaguars, elk, and prairie chickens also disappeared from Texas. Passenger pigeons, although existing at first in huge numbers, became extinct. They were easy to kill and were hunted for sport and food. Trees where they roosted, their habitat, were cut to clear the land for farming, with the result that the entire species disappeared. Black bears and ivory-billed woodpeckers were scared off into wilderness areas, while alligators, brown pelicans, and pronghorn antelope were all but killed off. Conservation programs in the 20th century have helped to increase the numbers of animals, but the future of whooping cranes, peregrine falcons, Ridley turtles, and southern bald eagles is uncertain.

Although some animals have disappeared, new ones have arrived in Texas. Beginning in the 15th century the Spanish brought horses, sheep, goats, pigs, and cattle to the land. Brown house sparrows multiplied from a flock released in Galveston in 1867. European starlings, another type of bird, landed first in New York in 1890. They flew westward and landed in Texas around 1925. The armadillo swam the Rio Grande in the 1840s; the grackle, a large black bird with a voice that sounds like its name, appeared in the 20th century; the fire ant marched into East Texas in the 1950s; the Asian tiger mosquito arrived in a shipment of old tires at the Port of Houston in 1985; and African killer bees swarmed into Texas from Mexico in 1990. The arrival and disappearance of these various species have affected the environment of Texas, but human beings have been the most important agents of change. Because of their technology the Spanish and the Americans have done the most to alter land and life in what is now the Lone Star State.

The Armadillo

The whimsical armadillo became a folk symbol for Texas in the 1960s, but has never been adopted as an official state animal. Its Spanish name means "little armored one." There are 20 kinds of armadillo in North and South America, but only the nine-banded species lives in Texas and the United States. Adults weigh about 14 pounds and measure 2 feet long. They are covered with a flexible, plate-like shell with nine parts that can fold like an accordion. The Texas armadillo cannot curl into a complete ball and depends upon running through brush and quick digging to escape from enemies. Their main foes are wolves, bobcats, mountain lions, coyotes, dogs, and automobiles.

Armadillos crossed the Rio Grande from Mexico in the 1840s and reached Nueces Bay in the 1890s. They waddled into Louisiana in the 1920s and have since spread through most of the South. They eat earthworms, crayfish, lizards, and insects, and nest in deep burrows along riverbanks. Humans have used armadillos for food, baskets, pets, and race animals. When grilled and seasoned with chili powder, paprika, salt, and catsup, "dillo" meat tastes like pork.

An armadillo drawn by American naturalist John Audubon in 1848.

With a map and a Bible in his hand, this Spanish priest typifies the dual role of explorer and missionary often performed by the first priests to arrive in Texas. This pen-and-ink drawing was done in the 1980s by José Cisneros, an artist known for his historically accurate depictions of Texas's early days.

Chapter Two

Texas and Spain

The stunning news of land to the west that Christopher Columbus announced in Spain in 1493 quickened the heartbeat of Europe. Explorers came rapidly—John Cabot, Vasco Núñez de Balboa, Fernando Magellan, Hernando Cortés, and others in search of gold, adventure, and a water route to the Far East. Columbus himself made three more voyages to the New World, still thinking that he was near China. He found the Indians, as he called the native inhabitants, quite amazing. Just as Columbus's voyages came about somewhat by error, so did the first contact between Europeans and Native Americans in Texas.

On a cold, miserable November day in 1528 the Karankawa Indians met white men from Spain face to face for the first time. These Europeans landed with a thump on the beach of Galveston Island. They were what was left of a large expedition sent to conquer Florida. Under the command of Pánfilo de Narváez, 400 men and 82 horses landed on the Gulf side of Florida. They explored the area around Tallahassee, looking for gold to steal, but discovered only angry Indians.

The army returned to the coast and found that their ships had abandoned them. Left alone and hungry, the men ate their horses and built some crude boats. Using their shirts for sails, they floated westward. Their thought was to follow the coastline until they reached Spanish settlements in Mexico. Along the way, some of the boats fell apart in rough water and the men drowned. Others simply disappeared.

Finally, the chill waves dumped about 80 or 90 of the men at various places on Galveston Island. Narváez was lost at sea and the second in command, Álvar Núñez Cabeza de Vaca, recorded: "As we drifted into shore, a wave caught us and heaved the barge a horseshoe-throw out of the water. The jolt when it hit brought the dead-looking men to. Seeing land at hand, they crawled through the surf to some rocks. Here we made a fire and parched some of our corn. We also found rain water. The men began to regain their senses, their locomotion, and their hope."

The weary shipwrecked men shortly discovered that they were on an island, and Karankawa Indians who were hunting on the island shortly discovered the Spaniards.

The erroneous report by Father Marcos de Niza that he had seen the fabled golden city of Cíbola inspired Francisco Vásquez de Coronado to lead an expedition of 300 soldiers to seek and claim the city for Spain.

The meeting was friendly. The white men gave the Indians gifts of bells and beads, and the Indians gave food in return.

Having recovered some of their strength, Cabeza de Vaca and his men tried to continue their journey. They loaded equipment, food, and clothing onto the boat and pushed away from the shore, only to have their hopes destroyed. The rough, cold water capsized the boat about 100 yards from land and three men drowned as the rest struggled back to the beach, naked and stripped of their possessions.

The Indians who had seen what happened at first sat down on the sand and cried for 30 minutes in sympathy. Then, after building four large fires along a pathway to keep the nude men warm, the Karankawas took them to their village. The Spaniards feared that they would be eaten, but instead the Indians gave them food, shelter, and an all-night dance in their honor.

The first contact between Europeans and Texas Indians was thus one of friendship and helpfulness, but it did not last. The Karankawas began to die from disease and blamed the newcomers. In addition, the Indians discovered that some of the shipwrecked men had eaten their own companions in order to survive. The Karankawas were shocked at such cannibalism. At first they thought of killing all the Spaniards, but instead they turned them into slaves and medicine men. Out of the 400 men of the expedition, only 4 lived to reach the Spanish settlements in Mexico. No wonder that Cabeza de Vaca, one of four survivors of the Narváez expedition, called Galveston the "Island of Doom."

There had been an earlier investigation of the Texas coast. In 1519 Alonso Alvarez de Piñeda, a Spanish explorer, sailed from Jamaica along the Gulf Coast and produced the first map of the Gulf of Mexico. Much later, in 1785–86, José de Evia, a Spanish naval officer, drew a more detailed map of the coastline from Florida to Mexico. The first European to cross Texas, however, was Cabeza de Vaca. He lived for six years as a slave and a trader for the Indians, who exchanged skins, seashells, flint, and ocher, a body paint of red and yellow. Finally, he and the three others, including Esteban, a black slave, escaped and trekked out of Texas into Mexico. The exact route is unclear, but Cabeza de Vaca reported seeing buffalo and hearing rumors of a rich Native American tribe somewhere to the north.

Cabeza de Vaca refused to guide a return expedition to search for gold but Esteban, since he was a slave, had no choice but to obey the orders of the authorities in Mexico City. Esteban scouted ahead of the expedition and demanded personal gifts and favors from the Indians. The Indians killed him, but Father Marcos de Niza, the leader of the expedition, returned to Mexico City to trumpet the exciting news that he had seen from a distance the golden cities of Cíbola. These seven magnificent cities of enormous wealth, according to legend, had been built by seven Portuguese bishops who had fled in the 8th century to avoid their enemy, the Moors. Supposedly, the cities lay somewhere in the west, but no one had ever seen them.

Fired with the thought of claiming a fabulous treasure, the viceroy of Mexico ordered Francisco Vásquez de Coronado to

ride forth and find it. In 1540 Coronado, in gleaming golden armor, led the march to the north, followed by 300 soldiers, several hundred Indian allies, flocks of sheep, and herds of cattle and horses. Father Marcos guided the entrada, or expedition of conquest, across the deserts and mountains.

They finally reached a large valley dotted with Indian adobe houses. The Indians attacked with rocks and arrows, and Coronado struck back with a cavalry charge. The Indians fled, but what Coronado had conquered was only a poor Pueblo village of stone and dried bricks. There was no Cíbola, no streets made of gold.

Coronado sent the shamed Father Marcos back to Mexico City, but the army stayed during the winter in the upper Rio Grande Valley and marched forward again in the springtime. An Indian nicknamed the Turk had told them about Gran Quivira, a place where Indians caught fish larger than horses and where the chief slept under a tree hung with golden bells tinkling in the breeze. The Turk led the way through New Mexico and mounted the high plains of the Llano Estacado. The Spaniards reached Palo Duro Canyon, where Coronado ordered most of the army back to the Rio Grande. He was beginning to doubt the Turk. With a small squad of soldiers and the Turk in chains, Coronado pushed on into Kansas. There he

discovered that Gran Quivira was only the straw huts of Wichita Indians.

Under torture, the Turk admitted that he had lied. The Spaniards then baptized him to save his soul, and strangled him. Disappointed and defeated, Coronado returned to his army at the Rio Grande, where he spent another winter. It was difficult because the Indians had been scared away and there was little food left for the marauding Spaniards. In 1542 an exhausted Coronado returned to Mexico City to report that although Texas might be rich in land it was poor in gold.

Meanwhile, another Spanish expedition explored across the American South. Hernando de Soto started in Florida in 1539 with 600 men; he died on the banks of the Mississippi River in 1542. Before his death he assigned leadership to Luis de Moscoso de Alvarado. There is some question about his route, but Moscoso raided Caddo villages, probably in East Texas. Moscoso then returned to the Mississippi River, built ships, and sailed with 100 Indian slaves to Mexico in 1543. His entrada, too, failed to discover any great wealth.

Without the possibility of finding gold there was little interest in further exploration. In 1543 the king banned expeditions that killed Indians. Through their explorations, however, the Spanish could claim a

The arrival of the Coronado expedition into Palo Duro Canyon. This mural hangs in the Panhandle-Plains Historical Museum in Canyon.

An expedition led by Hernando de Soto explored much of the American South, beginning in Florida in 1539. Although de Soto himself died before reaching Texas, members of his expedition raided Indian villages in East Texas before returning to Mexico in 1543.

vast territory that reached from Florida through Texas into Mexico. Beginning in the mid-16th century settlers gradually built ranches and small towns in the Rio Grande Valley. Texas was only a poor, outlying part of a Spanish Empire that stretched around the world. Its value was mainly as a shield to keep other European nations away from the valuable gold and silver mines of Mexico.

This indifferent attitude toward Texas was changed by the French explorer René-Robert Cavelier, Sieur de La Salle. He had followed other Frenchmen into the Great Lakes region and floated down the Mississippi River. In 1682 he claimed the great river and its branches for his king, Louis XIV. This meant that France and Spain had laid claim to some of the same land. La Salle understood that establishing a town at the mouth of the Mississippi River, where it empties into the Gulf of Mexico, would make it possible to control the use of the waterway. He returned to France, convinced his king about the value of the Mississippi, and received orders to establish a colony.

La Salle left France in 1684 with 280 settlers on four ships, but his effort failed. He lost one ship to Spanish raiders in the West Indies and landed at the wrong spot with the others. Perhaps by error—no one is certain today—La Salle chose Matagorda Bay in Texas rather than the mouth of the Mississippi. His colony, called Fort St. Louis, was troubled by hostile Indians, disease, and bad decisions. He wrecked two of his ships, and the third one deserted for home. After rebellious men shot and killed their leader by ambush, a few of the Frenchmen walked all the way to French settlements in Canada.

Several others joined local Indian groups and went to live in their villages; the rest died from disease and exposure. The Karankawas destroyed the houses of the settlement.

Spies told the Spanish about the expedition, but they did not know what had happened to La Salle and the colony. The Spanish thought that the French threatened their empire and sent out 10 different expeditions to get rid of them. They did not find the settlement until 1689, when the governor of Coahuila, Alonso de León, uncovered the ruins of Fort St. Louis and three skeletons. That was the end of the La Salle threat, but the Spanish remained alert to future French incursions.

While Alonso de León was in East Texas the Caddo Indians allowed him to send missionaries to them. Since Spain was interested not only in gold but also in the salvation of souls, Roman Catholic priests walked side by side with the Spanish explorers. The Franciscans, a special order established in the 13th century within the church, trained monks, or priests (called *padres* in Spanish), to work in the New World with the Native Americans. Their job was to tell Indians about Jesus Christ and to convert them to the Christian religion. Otherwise, the priests believed, a person most likely would go to hell.

The Franciscans, who worked in pairs or in small groups, were practical men. When they set up a mission, they built a church, cleared land, planted crops, and began handicraft work such as pot making and weaving. They gave small presents and food to curious Indians and then tried to tell them about Christ and Christianity. The king paid the

cost of the missions and so the priests often served a double purpose. They spread the ideas of Christian religion and also worked as agents of the crown. Through the church hierarchy, the priests reported on local conditions and represented the government when no military or political officials were available.

In the late 1500s Spanish missionaries and settlers moved into what is now New Mexico, and in the 1600s Franciscans explored Texas. In 1681 the padres, forced out of New Mexico by rebellious Indians, built Corpus Christi de las Isleta, a mission on the Rio Grande at Ysleta. It is now a part of modern El Paso and is the oldest surviving community in Texas.

The missions often failed; life was difficult in the Texas wilderness. Sometimes the Indian desire for missions was real, but sometimes the Indians wanted missions only to give them power against their enemies. This is what happened at San Saba, northwest of the San Antonio missions. The Lipan Apaches, who were being defeated by the Comanches, asked for a mission at San Saba. The unsuspecting padres gladly agreed. The Lipans, who cared little about Christianity, secretly hoped to get the Spanish to fight the Comanches—and they did.

In the spring of 1758 two thousand Comanches, painted red and black, arrived at the new mission. They were armed with bows, lances, and French muskets (guns). The priests happily rushed out to give them gifts of tobacco and beads, but they were met with war whoops and death. The Indians even cut off the head of one priest and played ball with it.

For punishment the Spanish government sent out an army of 600 soldiers with Indian allies led by Colonel Diego Ortiz de Parilla. He wantonly demolished a Tonkawa village on his march northward and then began an attack on a Wichita village near the Red River. There the Comanches and their Indian allies were waiting. The village was protected by a palisade, or wall of logs, with a ditch in front. The Indian horses were in a safe corral, and the Indians behind the wall had guns acquired from French traders. In the fight, Parilla's Indian allies fled. He had to fight his way out of an encirclement and retreat all the way back to Bexar, later called San Antonio. It was the worst defeat for the Spanish during their time in Texas.

As long as the Spanish had the technical advantage of weapons, they remained undefeated. Once the Indians were armed with the same weapons, particularly horses, guns, and iron for knives and arrow points, the Spanish lost their military advantage. The Spanish and other Europeans, however, had an invisible weapon that nobody understood at the time—disease.

Europeans carried epidemic diseases such as smallpox, measles, cholera, and typhoid to the New World. The carrier may have been sick at the time, did not know why, and infected others. An entire ship filled with people who got sick at sea might arrive in America to infect the people on shore.

A group of 280 settlers led by the French explorer René-Robert Cavelier, Sieur de La Salle landed at Matagorda Bay in Texas. The expedition was a total failure—plagued by hostile Indians and disease. In this 1834 painting, artist George Catlin depicts La Salle's party being greeted by Indians in 1686.

Artist José Cisneros here depicts a priest saying Mass for Indians in about 1629.

Populations in Europe had been exposed to such diseases for a long time and had developed some immunity, or resistance, so that they did not become quite as sick. Native Americans, however, had no immunity and entire villages tended to fall ill all at once. Therefore, there were few people well enough to tend the sick, to provide food and drink. This made the illness worse and only a small number survived, often as few as 10 percent.

Smallpox, for example, struck the Caddo Indians in 1690. They may have caught it from the Alonso de León expedition or from the priests who followed. Thereafter, the Caddos regularly suffered from epidemics of smallpox. By 1800 their population, once the largest among Native Americans, had declined to a few hundred families. Cholera, which had a mortality rate of 50 percent, also killed large numbers. This disease and typhoid spread through impure water. Thus the stationary farming tribes, such as the Jumanos and Caddos, were hurt the most. They tended to stay in one spot and unknowingly pollute their water supply with the disease. The Comanches, in contrast, regularly moved their camp when someone died and thus avoided water pollution and death.

As the tribes weakened, they turned to the Spanish and French to help them fight their traditional Indian enemies. But the more contact the Indians had with Europeans, the more dependent and sicker they became. Only the nomadic horse people of the plains escaped this tragic cycle.

The Spanish king ordered that East Texas be conquered by priests who would convert Indians to Christianity, and de León, the governor who had looked for La Salle, therefore responded quickly to the request by the Caddos for missionaries. For three years, from 1690 to 1693, priests led by Father Damian Massenet tried to run missions. They failed because of disease, floods, lack of food, and stubborn Indians. The Caddos chose to believe in two gods. There was the god who gave power to the Spanish. Then there was their old god who took care of the land. The Caddos would not go to church, learn prayers, or obey the priests. Sadly, Father Massenet burned his two missions and returned to Mexico. When they left the country, de León and the others abandoned their livestock and thus, without thinking about it, left them to expand over the Texas environment. Living on the rich grass of the prairies, the loose horses and cattle evolved into wild herds of mustang ponies and longhorn cattle.

In the early 18th century Louis Juchereau de Saint-Denis, a French trader from New Orleans and Natchitoches, led a joint French and Spanish effort to reestablish the East Texas missions. The French and Spanish were both Roman Catholic, and for the moment were at peace with each other. Saint-Denis crossed Texas several times between 1714 and 1716, probably following the Camino Real, a mission trail blazed in 1691. He helped the Spanish locate new mission sites in East Texas and then pursued an Indian trade from his post in Natchitoches.

At Bexar, the Spanish established a supply point that was midway between the new East Texas missions and the older posts on the Rio Grande. In 1718 the priests started construction of San Antonio de Valero, a mission that became the Alamo. It was the first of a series of missions along the San Antonio River. To protect them, the Spanish government also built a presidio, or military post, called San Antonio de Bexar. In order to grow crops of squash, pumpkins, corn, and beans, the padres constructed irrigation ditches called *acequias* to carry water from the river. This was one of the earliest irrigation projects in Texas and is still in use today.

To boost population, the Spanish governor in Texas asked the king to send colonists. Fifty-six settlers arrived at Bexar

Free Blacks in a White World

According to the census data, in 1836 there were about 5,000 slaves and 150 free blacks living in Texas. The slaves lived mainly as plantation laborers for the production of cotton and sugar, much like slaves in other parts of the American South. The free blacks were African Americans who had escaped slavery through birth in a free family, purchase of their own freedom, or manumission, the granting of freedom by masters or courts. Free blacks could do as they wished, and most of them were small farmers or farm workers. There were a few exceptions—the most famous of them William Goyens of Nacogdoches.

Goyens's father was an ex-slave who had won his freedom fighting in the American Revolution. His mother was white. Goyens, born in 1794, grew up in North Carolina near Cherokee Indians and moved to Texas in 1820. Although he may have been illiterate, he became rich as a skillful blacksmith, wagon builder, freight hauler, miller, farmer, gunsmith, slave trader, and innkeeper. In 1826, while on a business trip to Natchitoches, Louisiana, he was captured by a man who sought to sell him into slavery. To escape, Goyens turned over to his captor his own female slave and agreed to become one himself if he were allowed to continue trading. Upon his return to Nacogdoches, Goyens filed suit in the courts, gained an annulment of the agreement, and thus maintained his freedom.

Mexicans, Anglo-Americans, and Indians all trusted Goyens. Consequently, he became important as a person to mediate between these different groups. During the Texas Revolution, he worked as an interpreter for Sam Houston in negotiations with the Cherokees who had moved into East Texas. There was a danger that the Indians might join with Santa Anna against the Texans—the added strength of the Indians would have been disastrous for the cause of Texas independence. This was avoided with a treaty that promised the Indians land in East Texas, and the Cherokees remained neutral during the war.

Following the Revolution, Goyens increased his fortune by operating a sawmill and gristmill and by land trades. He built a two-story mansion four miles west of Nacog-doches, where he lived with his Anglo wife, Mary Pate Sibley, a widow whom he married in 1832. Despite the efforts of jealous neighbors to take away his wealth, Goyens successfully defended himself by hiring the best lawyers in Nacogdoches. At the time of his death in 1856, he owned more than 12,000 acres of land and was one of the wealthiest men in Texas.

William Goyens, a free black man born in 1794, gained success in a wide range of fields, including farming, wagon building, and freight hauling. When he died in 1856 he was one of the richest men in Texas.

PLANO DELA POBLACION.

A detail of the plan of the Villa de San Fernando de Bexar, which became the first official town in Texas in 1731.

in 1731 from the Canary Islands, Spanish possessions off the coast of North Africa. The colonists organized the Villa de San Fernando de Bexar, which became the first official town in Texas. The settlers elected a city council and an *alcalde,* a combination mayor, sheriff, and judge. San Fernando, which merged with the nearby Alamo and presidio to become San Antonio, was the only settlement in Texas at the time in which the citizens had some voice in their government. It was also the most successful Spanish settlement in Texas.

As a result of alliances in the Seven Years War (1756–1763), France gave to Spain its claims to the Louisiana Territory, a vast tract of land through the middle of what is now the United States, from the Mississippi River to the Rocky Mountains. Since Spain now controlled all of the Gulf Coast from Florida to Mexico, this event ended the French threat to the Spanish Empire in Texas. The Spanish government now considered the frontier missions unnecessary and expensive and closed them. Again the Spanish government abandoned East Texas, but Spanish settlers, refusing orders to leave, established Nacogdoches in 1779 at the site of one of the deserted missions. Shortly, this

town became almost as important as San Antonio.

In 1800, after 250 years of struggle, the population of the Spanish Empire in Texas amounted to about 5,000 people. They worked on ranches around the Rio Grande and lived in the small towns at Laredo, San Antonio, La Bahía (later called Goliad), and Nacogdoches. Except for a small presidio at La Bahía, the coastline was undefended. On the prairies above the Coastal Plain, the Apaches and Comanches roamed undefeated. Spanish control of Texas was weak, however, and consequently the country of New Spain, the overseas empire in America, became attractive to land-hungry people from the east.

The Peace of Paris, signed in 1783, ended the American Revolution and gave to the victorious United States of America territory that reached from the Atlantic Ocean west to the Mississippi River and from Georgia north to the St. Lawrence River. By secret treaty in 1800, the Louisiana Territory passed back to France from Spain, and in 1803 France sold it to the United States. These complex events doubled the size of the United States, fed the desire of Americans to move westward, and placed Spanish Texas on the border of the American South. For Americans, Texas, with its unoccupied lands, was a temptation that could not be ignored.

Americans were a restless people and very different from the Spanish. Starting in the early 17th century British groups founded colonies along the Atlantic coast, while Spain worked to settle the Southwest. The British colonial population grew quickly because of immigration and be-

This 1886 photograph shows a portion of an aqueduct built around 1725 to carry water to missions near San Antonio.

cause settlers had large families. Germans, French, Dutch, and Scandinavians crossed the Atlantic, along with the Scots, Irish, Welsh, and English from Great Britain. In 1619 the first African slaves came to the colonies, and thereafter black Africans became a minority part of the population. The immigrants brought customs that in turn melded into those of the colonies.

Americans were more English than anything else and brought English laws, language, styles, customs, and holidays. That is why they are sometimes called Anglo-Americans, the word *Anglo* meaning "English." Their break with Great Britain during the Revolution was an important precedent; they carried those revolutionary ideals into Texas, where they came into conflict with Spanish culture. In their Declaration of Independence they had rejected the idea that a king should rule. Instead, the Americans said that people should rule over themselves and exercise individual freedoms, such as religious freedom, the right to buy a farm, work the land, and use the crops as they wished. Americans moving westward carried with them these ideas about government and rights. Most were loyal to the United States and had chosen a Protestant religion.

In the 1790s adventuresome Americans arrived in the New Orleans area, where they worked at ranching and Indian trade. The border between the United States and Texas was uncertain and Spain did not have enough people in Texas to hold back the pioneers drifting across the leaky border. The government therefore authorized the use of *empresarios*. Such people were granted huge blocks of virgin land in the Coastal Plain to settle. In turn, these promoters subdivided the land, advertised, found families to immigrate, and sold the property. In this way, Spain hoped to hold Texas, but before much could be done the empire fell apart.

In 1808 Emperor Napoleon of France invaded Spain. Officials in New Spain now had no effective king to issue orders. In the confusion, rebels in the New World decided that this was a good time to strike for independence. Most of the nations of Latin America were established between 1809 and 1825. Spain, even after the defeat of Napoleon in Europe and the return of the king in 1814, was unable to stop them.

In Mexico, Father Miguel Hidalgo y Costilla called for independence in 1810. His effort failed, and he was later captured and executed by Spanish officials. Others, however, continued to rebel. In Texas the situation was confused by filibusters, people from the outside trying to overthrow the government. The most interesting was James Long, an ambitious American from Virginia who wanted to be the leader of a new nation in Texas. With 120 followers, he took over Nacogdoches in 1819, announced the independence of Texas, and

Jean Laffite: The Pirate of the Gulf

Jean Laffite was born in France to a Spanish mother and a French father. The family emigrated to America and in 1808 Laffite and his brother Pierre set up a smuggling base near New Orleans. They would take items stolen by pirates, sneak them to New Orleans, and sell them illegally. Jean became known as the "Pirate of the Gulf." After helping the United States in the War of 1812, the Laffite brothers built a pirate base on Galveston Island, where they supplied freebooters with food and gunpowder and bought what the pirates had stolen. Jean Laffite then resold the stolen goods, including slaves, for a profit.

He ruled tightly over the pirate camp of about 1,000 people and hanged sea captains who disobeyed his orders. He said that his ships attacked only Spanish vessels, even though Laffite was a Spanish secret agent. After the U.S. Navy forced Laffite to leave Galveston in 1821, he disappeared. How he died is unknown, but the best guess is that he died of a fever in the Yucatan in the 1820s.

Laffite's shadowy end created tales of buried treasure. One of the stories claimed that before he left Galveston Laffite was heard to mutter, "I have buried my treasure under the three trees." The trees were a landmark on the island, and after he had departed several men went to the three trees at night to dig up the treasure. Their shovels struck a box in the sand and they pried open the lid. There in the moonlight appeared the pale face and rigid body of the pirate's dead wife.

declared himself president. Spanish soldiers drove him across the Sabine River out of Texas, but he was back the next year at a fort on the Bolivar Peninsula across from Galveston Island.

Leaving behind his pregnant wife, Long and 52 men joined other rebels at La Bahía on the San Antonio River. Mexico gained its independence in 1821 and the new Mexican officials at La Bahía sent Long to Mexico City. They did not quite trust him and at the capital a guard shot and killed him—no one knows if it was murder or an accident. Meanwhile, at the fort on the Bolivar Peninsula, Jane Long, alone except for her black slave Kian, waited for news. With Kian's aid, she gave birth to a daughter, fired a cannon to scare away Karankawa Indians, flew a red petticoat for a flag, and fished the bay with an old hammock. In 1822 Long finally heard of her husband's death and moved on with a group of passing settlers. Since her daughter was the first baby born to Anglo-Americans in Texas, Jane Long became known as the "Mother of Texas." The title also celebrates her loyalty and toughness.

The new nation of Mexico faced the same problem as Spain. If Mexico hoped to hold on to Texas, it had to have more people living there. The empresario system thus continued. Settlers could buy land for about 2 cents an acre, provided they became Mexican citizens and Roman Catholics. Since land was selling for $1.25 an acre in the United States, Texas was a bargain.

Moses Austin started as an empresario with the Spanish. He died before much was accomplished, but his son, Stephen F. Aus-

tin, took up the project with Mexico. He agreed to settle 1,200 families in the Coastal Plain of the lower Brazos and Colorado rivers. Austin mapped out the farms, distributed the land, collected fees, and punished hostile Indians from his town, San Felipe de Austin. Noah Smithwick, who arrived in 1827, described the settlement: "Twenty-five or perhaps thirty log cabins strung along the west bank of the Brazos River was all there was of it, while the whole human population of all ages and colors could not have exceeded 200."

By 1834 about 9,000 people lived on Austin's land, and other empresarios followed his lead. Some settlers simply moved across the border of Texas and set up farms without permission. This flow of migrants, people seeking their own homesteads, was unstoppable. It was the front wave of the American westward movement, a folk movement that had begun with the founding of the first colonies. Now it had reached Texas, and by 1836 there were about 35,000 people there, a sevenfold increase in 20 years.

Most of the newcomers came from the southern United States, and they resisted Mexican law and Spanish customs. They continued to speak English and to practice Protestant religions. The Americans also brought black slaves with them, but the Mexican government opposed slavery and tried to stop it. The Americans in Texas had little respect for the Mexican government, moreover, and were quick to speak out against it. In such a situation there was likely to be trouble—and it came with the Texas Revolution.

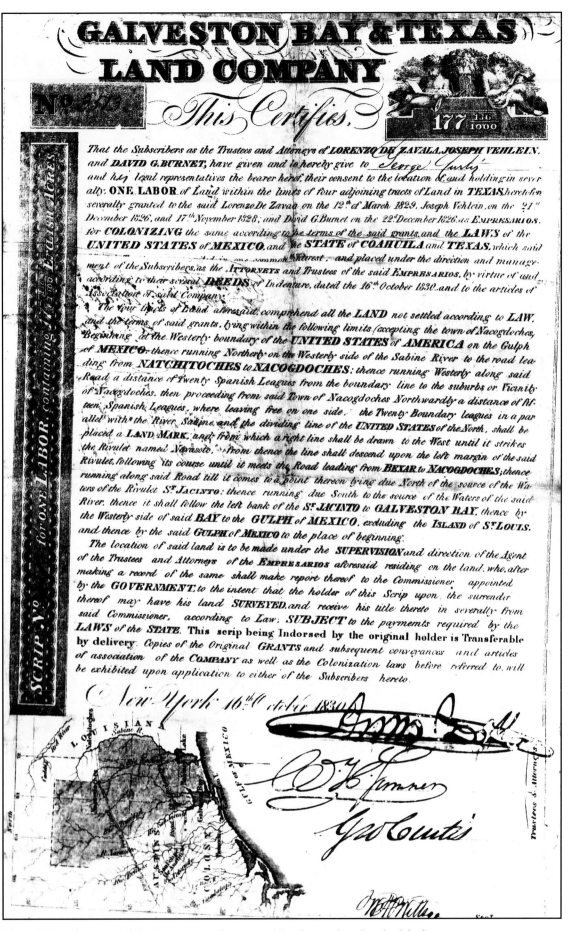

GALVESTON BAY & TEXAS LAND COMPANY

No.

This Certifies,

177 136/1000

That the Subscribers as the Trustees and Attorneys of **LORENZO DE ZAVALA, JOSEPH VEHLEIN,** and **DAVID G. BURNET,** have given and do hereby give to *George Curtis* and his legal representatives the bearer hereof, their consent to the location of and holding in severally, **ONE LABOR** of Land within the limits of four adjoining tracts of Land in **TEXAS,** heretofore severally granted to the said Lorenzo De Zavala on the 12th of March 1829, Joseph Vehlein, on the 21st December 1826, and 17th November 1828; and David G. Burnet on the 22d December 1826, as **EMPRESARIOS,** for **COLONIZING** the same according to the terms of the said grants, and the **LAWS** of the **UNITED STATES** of **MEXICO,** and the **STATE** of **COAHUILA** and **TEXAS,** which said _____ in one common interest, and placed under the direction and management of the Subscribers, as the **ATTORNEYS** and Trustees of the said **EMPRESARIOS,** by virtue of and according to their several **DEEDS** of Indenture, dated the 16th October 1830, and to the articles of Association of said Company.

The four tracts of Land aforesaid, comprehend all the **LAND** not settled according to **LAW,** and the terms of said grants, lying within the following limits (excepting the town of Nacogdoches, Beginning at the Westerly boundary of the **UNITED STATES** of **AMERICA** on the Gulph of **MEXICO,** thence running Northerly on the Westerly side of the Sabine River to the road leading from **NATCHITOCHES** to **NACOGDOCHES;** thence running Westerly along said Road a distance of Twenty Spanish Leagues from the boundary line to the suburbs or Vicinity of Nacogdoches, then proceeding from said Town of Nacogdoches Northwardly a distance of fifteen Spanish Leagues, where leaving free on one side the Twenty Boundary leagues in a parallel with the River Sabine, and the dividing line of the **UNITED STATES** of the North, shall be placed a **LAND MARK,** and from which a right line shall be drawn to the West until it strikes the Rivulet named Navasoto, from thence the line shall descend upon the left margin of the said Rivulet, following its course until it meets the Road leading from **BEXAR** to **NACOGDOCHES;** thence running along said Road till it comes to a point thereon being due North of the source of the Waters of the Rivulet St. **JACINTO;** thence running due South to the source of the Waters of the said River, thence it shall follow the left bank of the St. **JACINTO** to **GALVESTON BAY,** thence by the Westerly side of said **BAY** to the **GULPH** of **MEXICO,** excluding the **ISLAND** of St. **LOUIS,** and thence by the said **GULPH** of **MEXICO** to the place of beginning.

The location of said land is to be made under the **SUPERVISION** and direction of the Agent of the Trustees and Attorneys of the **EMPRESARIOS** aforesaid residing on the land, who, after making a record of the same shall make report thereof to the Commissioner appointed by the **GOVERNMENT,** to the intent that the holder of this Scrip upon the surrender thereof may have his land **SURVEYED,** and receive his title thereto in severalty from said Commissioner, according to Law; **SUBJECT** to the payments required by the **LAWS** of the **STATE.** This scrip being Indorsed by the original holder is Transferable by delivery. Copies of the Original **GRANTS** and subsequent conveyances and articles of association of the **COMPANY** as well as the Colonization laws before referred to, will be exhibited upon application to either of the Subscribers hereto.

New York 16th October 1830

SCRIP No. for ONE LABOR, containing 177 136/1000 English ACRES

This 1830 certificate entitled the bearer to enter the empresario's colony and purchase land for five cents per acre.

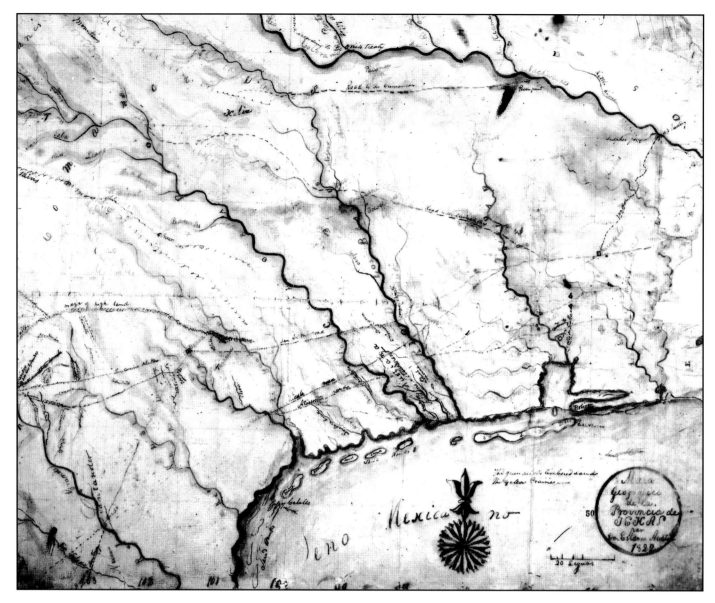

Stephen Austin (below) drew this map of southeastern Texas in 1822. He accurately depicted the roads he traveled in search of a site for his colony.

In 1829–30 the Mexican government freed the slaves, stopped immigration from the United States, and put a tax on goods imported from the U.S. over the Texas border. Anglo-Americans in Texas objected, and brief fighting broke out at Velasco and Anahuac. In 1832 and 1833 Texans met in conventions to discuss these problems and request changes from Mexico City. The Mexican government allowed colonists to keep their slaves, promised a revision of the customs taxes, and reopened immigration, but did not permit Texas to become a state with its own local government.

Changes in Mexico brought Antonio López de Santa Anna to power as dictator in 1835. He again ordered the collection of customs taxes, which sparked trouble at the small town of Anahuac on Trinity Bay. William B. Travis, a hot-headed lawyer from South Carolina, led a small band of citizens who freed prisoners arrested for smuggling. The Mexican government demanded that Travis and other rebels submit to a military trial, but the Texas colonists refused to allow that to happen. At this point Stephen F. Austin, who had gone to Mexico City to argue the settlers' case, returned to Texas and announced, "War is our only resource."

It started in October 1835. Mexican Colonel Domingo de Ugartechea of San Antonio ordered a patrol to take a cannon from the town of Gonzales. Andrew Ponton, the alcalde, refused to give it up. Ugartechea then sent a larger patrol, but when it arrived on October 2, 1835, with a written order for the gun, they faced a loaded cannon pointing at them and a band of 160 Texans flying a flag that read, "Come And Take It." The sides lined up, and the Texans fired. With no orders to attack and with one man dead, the Mexicans retreated to San Antonio. The war had begun.

Austin and others joined the Texans at Gonzales and marched toward San Antonio. On the way, they fought a brief battle at Mission Concepción. The Texans correctly feared the lances of the Mexican cavalry and took a defensive stand in the wooded curve of a river bank. The Mexicans' grapeshot, small iron balls shot from a cannon, ripped into the trees and showered the Texans with ripe pecans. Three times the Mexican soldiers charged into the deadly crossfire of the Kentucky long rifles carried by the Texans. Although untrained as soldiers, the Texans were skilled frontier hunters, and no one had to teach them how to shoot. After 30 minutes of fighting, the Mexicans retreated to San Antonio. They had lost 60 men; the Texans had lost only one.

Edward Burleson, a man with fighting experience, took charge of the Texas army and surrounded San Antonio. After a month of siege, a captured Mexican soldier revealed that General Martín Perfecto de Cós, who had reinforced the city, was about ready to surrender. Ben Milam, a 47-year-old scout and Indian trader, rallied the men with the challenge, "Who will go into San Antonio with old Ben Milam?" The assault lasted 5 days, and although Milam and three other Texans were killed, it succeeded and Cós surrendered. Burleson gave the Mexicans a parole with the promise that they would leave Texas and never return. It was a promise they would not keep.

Meanwhile, a revolutionary government, the Consultation, met at San Felipe. It sent Austin and others to the United States to rally support; appointed Henry Smith, an independence leader from Brazoria, to run the government; and assigned Sam Houston, a politician and soldier from Tennessee, to command the army. The 55 delegates were divided over the question of independence, however, and delayed this decision until March 1836, when they agreed to meet again. Then everything fell apart.

Houston withdrew from leadership after quarreling with the others about strategy and, instead, traveled to East Texas to prevent an alliance between Mexico and the Indians. Henry Smith argued with his advisers and was replaced by James Robinson, a lawyer from Nacogdoches. In San Antonio, Travis joined forces with James Bowie, a Louisiana frontiersman, who had been ordered by Houston to abandon the city. Bowie was sick with typhoid-pneumonia, and Travis took over full leadership. Travis, stubbornly, did not choose to leave, so contrary to orders the Texan force waited in the Alamo. At Goliad, James W. Fannin of Velasco, with another group of volunteer soldiers, also waited to see what would happen. Their inaction would prove to be fatal.

Santa Anna, meanwhile, marched northward with an army of 6,000 to put down the rebellion. Part of the army under General José Urrea turned on Goliad. Fannin foolishly left the shelter of the old presidio and retreated toward Victoria. He was too

General Santa Anna, shown here in an 1850 daguerreotype, led an army of 6,000 Mexican soldiers against 180 men in the Battle of the Alamo. He considered himself the "Napoleon of the West," even though he lost Texas in the Texas Revolution and was defeated in the Mexican-American War.

Sam Houston led the Texan army to victory at the decisive Battle of San Jacinto on April 21, 1836. He was later elected president of the Republic of Texas. When he died in 1863, his last words to his wife, Margaret, were, "Texas! Margaret! Margaret!"

slow, and Urrea surrounded the Texans on an open prairie. Fannin surrendered with the idea that his men would be sent on parole to the United States. Instead, eight days later, under orders from Santa Anna, firing squads marched the captives to an open field at dawn and shot 342 men of the Texas army. Twenty-eight managed to escape in the confusion of gunfire and smoke to tell this bloody tale of atrocity.

In the meantime, Santa Anna and the main part of the Mexican army marched into San Antonio. A few more men responded to Travis's famous letters to the Texas government asking for help. "I shall never surrender or retreat," he finally wrote, signing the letter "Victory or Death." The entire male population of Gonzales had arrived, and so had Davy Crockett, the famous Kentucky frontiersman. Their citadel included the Alamo mission and compound, which was enclosed with 9-foot-high walls, 21 pieces of artillery, and a clear field of fire in all directions. The Alamo garrison held more than 180 men when Santa Anna called for surrender. Travis answered with a cannon shot.

The Mexican infantry, lacking the help of Santa Anna's siege cannons, which had failed to reach the city, charged with ladders to climb the walls. Mexican bugles sounded the *Deguello*, announcing no mercy. The Texans repelled the attack with rifle and artillery fire. As his men faltered and fell, Santa Anna threw in his reserve soldiers, who scrambled up the ladders to engage the Texans in hand-to-hand combat on the walls. Travis died early in the battle with a bullet in his brain; Bowie died fighting in his sickroom; Davy Crockett suffered capture and execution. It was over in 90 minutes. Most of the people in the Alamo

were killed, except Suzanna Dickenson, her daughter, Travis's black slave Joe, and several family members of Mexicans from San Antonio who had chosen to side with the defenders. Santa Anna released these people to carry the news of the Texan defeat.

Santa Anna lost 600 men, including some of his best troops, particularly sergeants and corporals. In addition he gave his enemy a cause for ferocious revenge. Forever after, the cries of "Remember the Alamo!" and "Remember Goliad!" have echoed in the halls of Texas history. The Texans lost valuable men and gained little.

Santa Anna had not been stopped and the fighting continued.

Although the men at Goliad and San Antonio did not know it, on March 2, 1836, the Consultation met again and declared Texas independent. The delegates went on to write a constitution which gave each family in Texas 4,605 acres of land and made slavery legal. The form of government was similar to that of the United States, with a president, two-part congress, and supreme court. David G. Burnet, an empresario who had once fought for Venezuelan independence from Spain, was named temporary president and Sam Hous-

In 1885 Theodore Gentilz painted this view of the attack on the Alamo. The Mexican army can be seen advancing from all sides on the greatly outnumbered, yet still defiant, Texans.

ton again assigned leadership of the Texan army. This time, with Bowie, Travis, and Fannin gone, there was no challenge to his command.

Houston galloped toward San Antonio and found 400 men waiting for him at Gonzales. Suzanna Dickenson told him about the fate of the Alamo and he learned of the slaughter at Goliad. Worse, Santa Anna was in pursuit, and Texas independence was in mortal danger. Houston ordered Gonzales burned and began a retreat. He got as far as the Colorado River. There he paused and drilled the men in military movements, and retreated further. At the Brazos River he paused again to train his ragtag army. Although the restless men wanted to fight, Houston ordered retreat. Eastward toward the Sabine River, the boundary of Texas, he retreated.

The Anglo-American settlers cursed Houston for cowardice, rushed from their homes, and fled ahead of the army. This was called the "Runaway Scrape." The roads were muddy, the air chill, the streams flooding with icy water. Pioneer Mary Rabb wrote, "We was all drove out of ouer houses with ouer little ones to suffer with cold and hungry, and little Lorenzy not three months when we started died on the road."

President Burnet moved the government from Harrisburg to Galveston Island so that he could escape to New Orleans if necessary, and he tried to get Houston to fight. "You must retreat no farther," he wrote. "The country expects you to fight. The salvation of the country depends on you doing so." Still, Houston retreated.

Santa Anna mistook Houston's actions for fear and thought Houston would withdraw all the way out of Texas across the Sabine River. So, with a part of his army, Santa Anna tried to capture the Texas government at Harrisburg. He failed, but burned the town anyway. The two armies, now close together, were about the same size and they set up camps on opposite sides of a small prairie called San Jacinto. The prairie bordered Buffalo Bayou, close to the present site of Houston.

For Sam Houston and his men, the time of reckoning was at hand. There was a brief skirmish on April 20, 1836. The next morning General Cós arrived with 542 tired, hungry soldiers to aid Santa Anna. The Mexican force now numbered about 1,600; the Texan army counted 900. Santa Anna allowed the men to sleep and rest and, underestimating the Texans, he posted only a small guard.

At siesta time on April 21, 1836, Houston led his men into battle. They advanced on the run in a single rank 1,000 yards long across the open field. They were hidden by a small rise in the land until they were almost upon the Mexican encampment. Then two cannons, the "Twin Sisters," fired broken horseshoes and small sharp bits of metal straight into the Mexican tents. A four-piece band of three fifers and one drummer broke into the popular Texas song, "Will You Come to the Bower I Have Shaded for You?" The Texans fell upon the camp screaming "Remember the Alamo!" and "Remember Goliad!"

Most of the surprised Mexican soldiers fled in panic, but some fought courageously—and died. Santa Anna and his staff tried to hide in nearby woods. The Texans won the battle in 18 minutes, but a slaughter with guns, Bowie knives, and swords continued afterward. The Texan soldiers refused to stop, and the grass of San Jacinto dripped with blood. A rider galloped after the refugees of the "Runaway Scrape" and shouted out, "Turn back! Turn back! The Texian army has whipped the Mexicans! Turn back!"

The Texans lost 9 men killed and 34 wounded, including Houston, who had been shot in the right leg just above the ankle. The Mexican army suffered 630 killed, 208 wounded, and 730 captured,

The Bowie Knife

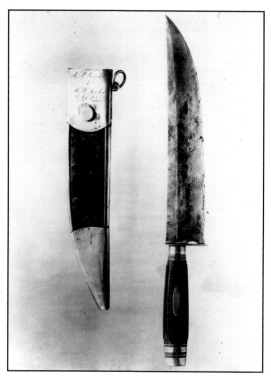

This example of a Bowie knife is more than 14 inches long and is on display in the Alamo museum.

James Bowie

James Bowie was born in 1796 in Kentucky. At the age of 19 he moved to Louisiana, where he bought slaves from the pirate Jean Laffite at one dollar per pound. Bowie smuggled the slaves to New Orleans for resale. According to one story, he designed his famous knife while recovering from a gunshot wound. In another version his brother gave him the knife. By all accounts he became a notorious knife fighter.

In 1827, Bowie was involved in a brawl on a Mississippi sandbar. He was hurt and lying on the sand when an enemy charged him with a small sword carried inside a cane. Bowie lurched to his feet as his opponent lunged at him. He caught the sword with one hand and jerked the man in close. With his knife he gutted his enemy and twisted the blade "to cut his heart strings," as Bowie later told the story. Thereafter, Jim Bowie was a legend and the Bowie knife became a favorite frontier weapon, because it was more reliable than the flintlock pistols of the day, which were likely to misfire. After his mother heard about his death at the Alamo, she said, "I'll wager no wounds were found in his back."

The knife was like a large, heavy butcher knife, with a handle made of horn. Some people called it a small sword, but it could be thrown, and the strong 10-inch blade would not break. It was used for skinning, cutting up meat, eating, fighting, hammering, and, some said, for picking the teeth.

In this 1844 painting, made eight years after the famous battle, artist Theodore Gentilz painted the Alamo as it lay in ruins.

At the end of the 19th century, the Alamo was threatened with destruction, and the site was used for a hotel. The photo at top, from 1898, shows a bustling Alamo Plaza with streetcars and horse-drawn carriages. The photo at bottom, from 1900, shows one of the Alamo Plaza saloons.

No one knows how the old mission got its name. In Spanish the word "Alamo" means "cottonwood." Perhaps it was named for a grove of cottonwoods nearby, or maybe by Spanish soldiers of Alamo del Parras in Coahuila, Mexico, who camped there during the Mexican Revolution. The Alamo began as the San Antonio de Valero Mission, founded by Father Antonio de Olivares in 1718. The mission was built in typical Franciscan style, with a large rectangular courtyard, or plaza, covering three acres and surrounded by a stone wall 3 feet thick and 9 feet high. Against three of these walls and facing into the plaza were small adobe rooms, while against the fourth, eastern, wall were a two-story convent and the Alamo chapel. Several large gates opened into the courtyard.

Missionary activity later declined, the roof of the chapel collapsed around 1762, and the site was abandoned in 1793. The empty buildings at the mission were used by Mexican soldiers from 1821 to 1835, but they surrendered during the Texas Revolution when "Old Ben" Milam led an attack on the city. Shortly afterward it became a fortress for the Texans. Although destined for eventual restoration as the main feature of the fortress, the chapel at the time of Santa Anna's attack was without a roof and littered with debris. Still, with walls 4 feet thick and 22 feet high the chapel became the last refuge for the besieged defenderss. Following the assault the Alamo was in ruins.

Various owners later made changes and partial restorations to the buildings and surroundings.

In 1883 the State of Texas bought the Alamo from the Roman Catholic Church and gave it to the City of San Antonio. In 1905 the city donated it to the Daughters of the Republic of Texas, an historical society that continues to take care of it. The Alamo, in the heart of downtown San Antonio, is considered a revered place of the Texas Revolution and attracts 3 million tourists each year. In 1994 it became the focal point of a local political fight concerning control of the site, expansion of the grounds, and the museum's presentation of Mexican participation in the battle. The Alamo is important, however, not only as a historical reminder of what happened in 1836, but also because it asks all visitors an important question— for what purpose would you sacrifice your life?

This early 20th-century painting, Chili Queens at the Alamo, shows a chili stand on Alamo Plaza. Such stands were once a tradition on Alamo Plaza and other plazas throughout San Antonio.

In 1905, the City of San Antonio granted control of the Alamo to the Daughters of the Republic of Texas. Under their leadership, the Alamo has become one of the most popular tourist attractions in the state.

including Santa Anna. He was identified by his men the next day while trying to disguise himself as a private in his own army. Utterly defeated, Santa Anna instructed the remaining Mexican soldiers to leave Texas. Although they could have continued the fight, the Mexican forces slowly withdrew from the new nation, the Republic of Texas.

While Houston traveled to New Orleans for the treatment of his injured leg, President Burnet signed the Treaty of Velasco with Santa Anna. This treaty gave Texas its independence, but Mexican senators rejected the treaty and promised to continue the war. For them it was unfinished business and Texas was a rebellious province. Because they did not renew the fighting, however, Texas was free.

Thus ended Hispanic dominion in Texas, but the influence of the Spanish heritage continued. In the following years Texans adopted the techniques of the cattle industry started by the Spanish, such as using tough range cows and cattle brands. They continued irrigated farming around San Antonio. Spanish architecture remained popular, as did Mexican food. Spanish place names were kept—places like San Antonio, Gonzales, El Paso, Rio Grande, and Brazos. The Roman Catholic religion endured, and the Alamo became a revered place for all Texans.

Still, the Texas Revolution created bitter memories. Hispanics, or Mexican Americans as they were later called, became a distrusted minority. They frequently lived apart from the rest of society, had no political power, and were almost faceless in Texas society until the middle of the 20th century. The Spanish imprint, however, was indelible even though it was hardly noticed in the new land of the Anglo-Americans.

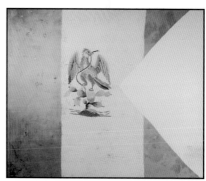

At the Battle of San Jacinto on April 21, 1836, the Texas army led by Sam Houston routed Santa Anna's Mexican forces. The Texans captured 730 Mexican soldiers, including Santa Anna himself. They also captured this Mexican battle flag.

The Unanimous
Declaration of Independence
made by the
Delegates of the People of Texas
in General Convention
at the Town of Washington
on the 2nd day of March 1836

When a government has ceased to protect the lives, liberty and property of the people, from whom its legitimate powers are derived, and for the advancement of whose happiness it was instituted, and, so far from being a guarantee for the enjoyment of those inestimable and inalienable rights, becomes an instrument in the hands of evil rulers for their oppression. When the Federal Republican Constitution of their country, which they have sworn to support, no longer has a substantial existence, and the whole nature of their government has been forcibly changed, without their consent, from a restricted federative republic, composed of sovereign states, to a consolidated central military despotism, in which every interest is disregarded but that of the army and the priesthood, both the eternal enemies of civil liberty, the everready minions of power, and the usual instruments of tyrants. When, long after the spirit of the constitution has departed, moderation is at length, so far lost by those in power, that even the semblance of freedom is removed, and the forms themselves of the constitution discontinued; and so far from their petitions and remonstrances being regarded, the agents who bear them are thrown into dungeons, and mercenary armies sent forth to force a new Government upon them at the point of the bayonet. When, in consequence of such acts of malfeasance and abduction, on the part of the government, anarchy prevails, and civil society is dissolved into its original elements. In such a crisis, the first law of nature, the right of self preservation—the inherent and inalienable rights of the people to appeal to first principles and take their political affairs into their own hands in extreme cases, enjoins it as a right towards themselves and a sacred obligation to their posterity to abolish such Government and create another in its stead, calculated to rescue them from impending dangers, and to secure their future welfare and happiness.

Nations, as well as individuals, are amenable for their acts to the public opinion of mankind. A statement of a part of our grievances is, therefore, submitted to an impartial world, in justification of the hazardous but unavoidable step now taken of severing our political connection with the Mexican people, and assuming an independent attitude among the nations of the earth.

The Mexican Government by its colonization laws invited and induced the Anglo-American population of Texas to colonize its wilderness under the pledged faith of a written Constitution, that they should continue to enjoy that constitutional liberty and republican government to which they had been habituated in the land of their birth, the United States of America. In this expectation they have been cruelly disappointed, inasmuch as the Mexican nation has acquiesced in the late changes made in the Government by General Antonio Lopez de Santa Anna, who having overturned the constitution of his country, now offers us the cruel alternative, either to abandon our homes acquired by so many privations, or submit to the most intolerable of all tyranny, the combined despotism of the sword and the priesthood.

It has sacrificed our welfare to the State of Coahuila, by which our interests have been continually depressed through a jealous and partial course of legislation carried on at a far distant seat of government by a hostile majority, in an unknown tongue, and this too, notwithstanding we have petitioned in the humblest terms, for the establishment of a separate state government, and have, in accordance with the provisions of the national constitution, presented to the general Congress a republican constitution, which was, without just cause contemptuously rejected.

It incarcerated in a dungeon, for a long time, one of our citizens, for no other cause but a zealous endeavor to procure the acceptance of our constitution and the establishment of a state government.

It has failed and refused to secure on a firm basis, the right of trial by jury, that palladium of civil liberty, and only safe guarantee for the life, liberty, and property of the citizen.

It has failed to establish any public system of education, although possessed of almost boundless resources (the public domain) and although it is an axiom, in political science, that unless a people are educated and enlightened it is idle to expect the continuance of civil liberty, or the capacity for self government.

It has suffered the military Commandants stationed among us to exercise arbitrary acts of oppression and tyranny; thus trampling upon the most sacred rights of the citizen, and rendering the military superior to the civil power.

It has dissolved by force of arms, the State Congress of Coahuila and Texas, and obliged our representatives to fly for their lives from the seat of government, thus depriving us of the fundamental political right of representation.

It has demanded the surrender of a number of our citizens, and ordered military detachments to seize and carry them into the Interior for trial, in contempt of the civil authorities, and in defiance of the laws and the Constitution.

It has made piratical attacks upon our commerce, by commissioning foreign desperadoes, and authorizing them to seize our vessels, and convey the property of our citizens to far distant ports for confiscation.

It denies us the right of worshipping the Almighty according to the dictates of our own conscience, by the support of a national religion calculated to promote the temporal interest of its human functionaries rather than the glory of the true and living God.

It has demanded us to deliver up our arms, which are essential to our defence, the rightful property of freemen, and formidable only to tyrannical governments.

It has invaded our country, both by sea and by land, with intent to lay waste our territory, and drive us from our homes, and has now a large mercenary army advancing, to carry on against us a war of extermination.

It has, through its emissaries, incited the merciless savage, with the tomahawk and scalping knife, to massacre the inhabitants of our defenceless frontiers.

It has been, during the whole time of our connection with it, the contemptible sport and victim of successive military revolutions, and hath continually exhibited every characteristic of a weak, corrupt, and tyrannical government.

These, and other grievances, were patiently borne by the people of Texas, until they reached that point at which forbearance ceases to be a virtue. We then took up arms in defence of the national Constitution. We appealed to our Mexican brethren for assistance. Our appeal has been made in vain. Though months have elapsed, no sympathetic response has yet been heard from the Interior. We are, therefore, forced to the melancholy conclusion that the Mexican people have acquiesced in the destruction of their liberty, and the substitution therefor of a military government—that they are unfit to be free and incapable of self government.

The necessity of self preservation, therefore, now decrees our eternal political separation.

We, therefore, the delegates, with plenary powers, of the people of Texas, in solemn convention assembled, appealing to a candid world for the necessities of our condition, do hereby resolve and declare that our political connection with the Mexican nation has forever ended, and that the people of Texas do now constitute a free, Sovereign, and independent Republic, and are fully invested with all the rights and attributes which properly belong to independent nations, and, conscious of the rectitude of our intentions, we fearlessly and confidently commit the issue to the decision of the Supreme Arbiter of the destinies of nations.

Richard Ellis, President
of the Convention & Delegate
from Red River

Charles B. Stewart   Sam Houston
Thos. Barnett   Edwin Waller
                            Asa Brigham

John S. D. Byrom   Geo. C. Childress
Francis Ruis   Bailey Hardeman
J. Antonio Navarro   Thomas Jefferson Rusk
Jesse B. Badgett   Robert Potter
Wm. D. Lacy   Charles Taylor
William Menefee   John S. Roberts
Jn. Fisher   Collin McKinney
Matthew Caldwell   Albert H. Latimer
William Motley   James Power
Lorenzo de Zavala   Sam Houston
Stephen H. Everitt   David Thomas
Geo. W. Smyth   Edwin Conrad
Elijah Stapp   Martin Parmer
Claiborne West   Edwin O. Legrand
Wm. B. Scates   Stephen W. Blount
M. B. Menard   Jas. Gaines
A. B. Hardin   Wm. Clark Jr.
J. W. Bunton   Sydney O. Pennington
Tho. J. Gazley   Wm. Carroll Crawford
R. M. Coleman   Jno. Turner
Sterling C. Robertson

Benjamin Briggs Goodrich
G. W. Barnett
James G. Swisher
Jesse Grimes
S. Rhoads Fisher
John W. Moore
John W. Bower
Saml. A. Maverick from Bejar
Sam P. Carson
A. Briscoe
J. B. Woods   Test: H. S. Kimble Secretary

Chapter Three

The Lone Star: Nation and State

The Texas Declaration of Independence, which established the independent Republic of Texas, free from Mexican control, was signed on March 2, 1836. The authors used Thomas Jefferson's Declaration of Independence as a model.

After treatment for the wounds he suffered at the Battle of San Jacinto, Sam Houston returned from New Orleans and the voters of Texas elected him president of the Republic. The term was three years; presidents could not serve two terms in a row, according to the new constitution. People in Texas still hoped that the United States would agree to annex Texas, and several lobbyists, led by Anson Jones, traveled to Washington, D.C. Houston even sent Santa Anna, the defeated dictator of Mexico, who had agreed to help. All failed.

For the moment the politicians of the United States refused. They were opposed because those who wanted to abolish slavery did not want a large new slave area to deal with. Also, it was feared that annexation would cause a war with Mexico. The Texans would have to wait. On his last day in office U.S. President Andrew Jackson signed the bill that recognized the independence of Texas. In friendship he invited the Texas agents to the White House in his final hours. Jackson raised a wine glass to them in salute and said, "Gentlemen, the Republic of Texas." Then he remembered his old friend Sam Houston and gave another salute: "The President of the Republic of Texas."

Houston, meanwhile, had problems to solve. The worst difficulty was to find money to run the government. The soldiers who had fought the war had been promised 320 acres of land for each three months' time in the service. Houston released most of the army and gave them their land. In order to increase the population, immigrants were also promised land, so between 1837 and 1841 the government gave away over 1 million acres. This meant that the government could not make much money from selling the new republic's greatest asset.

The government was able to get some income from customs taxes, fees, poll taxes for voting, and licenses. There was never enough to pay the costs, however, so the government created money simply by printing it. Such paper money was valuable only when people thought that the government was strong. By the end of Houston's first term in office, the "star money," so called because of a five-pointed star printed on the face of the bill, had decreased in value to a

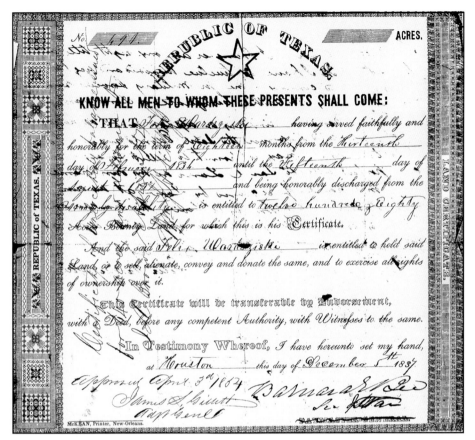

This $50 bill, printed by the Republic of Texas in 1840, was worth only 2 cents in U.S. money.

where, wanted the Cherokees and all Indians to leave. Houston, who had lived with the Cherokees in 1829 and was a friend of the Indians, lamented, "If I could build a wall from the Red River to the Rio Grande so high that no Indian could scale it, the white people would go crazy trying to devise a means to get beyond it."

Houston was helpless. The next president, Mirabeau B. Lamar, a poet who had led the cavalry at the Battle of San Jacinto, cared little for the Cherokees or other Indians. After taking office late in 1838 Lamar announced that "the white man and the red man cannot dwell in harmony together" and ordered the Texas Rangers, a frontier police unit mounted on horseback, to protect white frontier areas. "I experience no difficulty in deciding on a proper policy to be pursued towards them (Indians)," Lamar said. "It is to push a vigorous war against them . . . without mitigation or compassion." He told the Cherokees they had no valid claim to land in Texas and offered to pay the costs of their removal from the Republic. Talks failed, the Indians refused to leave, and the Cherokee War started in 1839.

Five hundred soldiers marched into East Texas, where they attacked and burned Indian cornfields and villages. At the Battle of the Neches near Tyler, in July, Chief Bowles died, wearing the sword and sash presented to him by Sam Houston. The soldiers scalped the body, tore the skin off the back, and left it to rot on the battlefield.

After a hundred warriors had died in the fighting, the Cherokees fled. John Bowles, the son of the chief, tried to lead a band

point where 1 dollar of Texas money was worth only 12 cents in U.S. money.

Houston also had a problem with the Cherokee Indians. The tribe originally came from the southern Allegheny Mountains in the eastern United States, but had been pushed westward by the Anglo-American frontier. In 1819–20 the Cherokees, led by Chief Philip Bowles, were pushed into East Texas, where they hoped to settle. In 1836, during the Texas Revolution, they agreed to a treaty with Sam Houston that gave them the right to stay. After the Revolution, the Texas Senate refused to honor the treaty because the Anglo-American settlers in Texas, like those else-around the troops to Mexico, but he was caught and killed at San Saba, where the Texans also captured 27 women and children. The rest of the Cherokees headed northward into Arkansas and eventually to Oklahoma. As the last of the Indians crossed the Red River, white hunters shot four of them. That was their farewell to Texas. Their land in East Texas was now open for Anglo-American settlement.

This episode is only a small part of the story of Indians in the United States. Wherever the Anglo-American frontier pushed westward, the shattered tribes retreated in front of it. Before 1800 a part of the Alabama tribe crossed the Sabine River into Texas and seven years later their kinfolk, the Coushattas, joined them. They were followed by bands of Choctaws, Shawnees, Delawares, Biloxis, Kickapoos, Quapaws, and the Cherokees. Many were peaceful farmers. Some had schools, practiced Christianity, planted cotton, and owned slaves, just like other pioneers. Only the Alabama-Coushattas were allowed to stay in East Texas. In 1854 the Texas legislature gave them a 1,300-acre reservation in Polk County, where they still live today.

Both sides had stories to tell about hundreds of small, bloody fights. In 1835 near Belton, for example, a raiding party of 11 Indians attacked the Taylor family. Their dog barked a warning before dying of a lance wound. Mrs. Taylor rushed the children into one room of their log house. After she and her husband shot two Indians as they tried to break in, other Indians set the roof on fire. The father wanted to surrender, but the mother climbed onto the rafters to save her home. As her daughters handed her buckets of milk and vinegar, the only liquids available, she put out the fire.

The Pig War

In 1839, France appointed Count Alphonse Dubois de Saligny as ambassador to Texas. He moved to Austin the next year and built the French Legation, which was to serve as his office and residence. Saligny got into trouble, however, because he did not pay his debts and tried to use fake money. He was also bored with Texas and decided to raise roses on the legation grounds, but a loose pig broke into the area and uprooted the plants. Saligny ordered a servant to kill the pig. The owner of the dead pig then had some men break into the legation and beat up his servant.

Saligny was furious and went to see President Sam Houston to demand payment for damages. Houston laughed at the story and refused. Saligny then promised that Texas would not get the large French loan that it wanted. The legation closed and Saligny went home to France, where he turned in an unfavorable report. The Republic of Texas did not get the loan.

The legation was sold several times and became state property in 1949. It is one of the oldest houses in Austin and an attraction for tourists and school excursions.

In 1858, 12-year-old Julia Robertson painted this portrait of the legation. Members of the Robertson family lived there from 1848 until 1940.

The struggle to drive the Comanches out of Texas and onto reservations in Oklahoma lasted many years.

In one of the most famous fights, a band of 100 Comanches, Kiowas, and Caddos rode up to the Parker Fort near the head of the Navasota River in 1836 while most of the Anglo men were away working in the fields. When the Parkers refused to give them a cow, the Indians attacked. They killed and scalped old John Parker and six others. They stripped Granny Parker of clothing and pinned her to the ground with a lance. She lived. When the Indians left they carried off two women and three children. Eventually, scouts were able to buy back four of the captives, but the other, a nine-year-old girl named Cynthia Ann Parker, grew up with the Comanches.

From the Anglo-American point of view the Indians were in the way and had no right to the land. From the Indian point of view the Anglo-Americans were invaders, but because most of the Indians did not write there are only a few accounts that state how they felt. Noah Smithwick, an early settler, recalled this conversation with an old Comanche:

> We have set up our lodges in these groves and swung our children from these boughs from time immemorial. When game beats away from us we pull down our lodges and move away, leaving no trace to frighten it, and in a little while it comes back. But the white man comes and cuts down the trees, building houses and fences, and the buffalo get frightened and leave and never come back, and the Indians are left to starve, or, if we follow the game, we trespass on the hunting ground of other tribes and war ensues. . . . No, the Indians were not made to work. If they build houses and try to live like white men they will all die.

The Taylors then killed another Indian and wounded two more. One of these ran to the wall of the cabin and peered through a hole. Mrs. Taylor saw him and threw a shovelful of hot coals from the fireplace in his face. "Take that, you yellow scoundrel," she said. The Indians then gave up the attack.

The Lone Star Flag

Six flags have flown over Texas as symbols of the nations that have ruled—Spain, France, Mexico, Texas Republic, Confederate States of America, and the United States. The Lone Star Flag of the Texas Republic resulted from a committee that designed the emblem in 1838. It was accepted by the Congress and President Lamar in 1839. The law said that the flag should have a vertical blue stripe at one end that was one-third the length of the flag and have a five-pointed white star in the center. The rest of the flag was to be two stripes of equal size—the one on top was to be white, the one on the bottom was to be red. After joining the United States the flag of the Republic became the state flag as well.

The idea of a lone star goes back to James Long. When he took over Nacogdoches he raised a red and white flag with a star. During the Revolution several other lone star flags appeared and Sarah Dodson made a flag at Harrisburg in 1835 that displayed a white star as the symbol of rising liberty. In the state song it is referred to as the "star of destiny."

The Lone Star Flag was adopted by the Republic of Texas in 1839. This flag is still flown today all across the state.

The war against the Comanches lasted a long time. When Lamar became president in 1838, Comanche raids on the frontier were frequent and the Texas Congress sent troops of Texas Rangers and volunteers to stop them. In 1840 the Comanches asked for a peace council at San Antonio, and it was granted. The Indians were supposed to bring in all their white captives, but they brought only one. The disappointed Texans then tried to capture the Indian chiefs, and angry fighting erupted. Seven whites and 35 Indians died.

It was a blunder. When the other Comanches heard about the "Council House Fight," as it was called, they killed about a dozen white prisoners in their villages and raided Victoria and Linnville. As the warriors retreated with their loot, they fought a Texan force at Plum Creek and lost 100 men. In the fall, Texans surprised a Comanche village on the Colorado River, where they killed 130 more Indians and recovered the property stolen from Linnville. After these events, the Comanches retreated westward and the frontier remained quiet for several years.

President Lamar also acted aggressively against Mexico. He tried and failed three times to obtain recognition of Texas independence. Following that, he formed a brief alliance with the Yucatan state of Mexico, where rebels wanted help from the Texas navy. The navy cleared the Gulf of Mexican ships and captured the town of Tabasco, but there were no lasting results.

Lamar also encouraged an expedition to Santa Fe, which the Texas Congress considered to be a part of Texas. In 1841 a group of 270 merchants and adventurers, along with 3 official agents of the Texas government, struggled 1,300 miles across the southern high plains of the Llano Estacado. When they got close to Santa Fe, Mexican troops easily captured the hungry and exhausted men and took them to prison in Mexico City. Most were released after a year, but José Navarro, one of the officials, remained a prisoner until 1844.

The wars against the Indians and the dealings with Mexico were expensive, and the Republic did not have enough money to pay for them. It was also costly to move the capital from Houston to Austin, Texas. Lamar did not like living in a town named for his rival, Sam Houston, and preferred to create a new capital on the frontier. It was named for the early Texas empresario Stephen F. Austin. To pay the costs, the Lamar government borrowed funds and printed more paper money, with the same poor results as before. Under Houston the Republic owed $2 million; under Lamar, the debt grew to $7 million.

Late in 1841 the voters elected Sam Houston president once again, but Lamar had unleashed financial demons that Houston had to control. To reduce costs Houston

Edward Johns, a midshipman in the Texas navy, drew these sketches on the cover of one of the journals he kept while at sea on the Austin.

In 1843, Texans seeking plunder drifted down the Rio Grande in four boats, to the Mexican town of Mier. This unauthorized raid ended in disaster for the Texans. Charles McLaughlin, a member of the expedition, sketched the group's crossing of the Rio Grande.

tried to sell the ships of the Texas navy. He was unable to do that—the people of Galveston, the home port, objected—and eventually the ships became a part of the United States Navy when Texas joined the United States. Mexico, moreover, in response to Lamar's aggressiveness, sent three armed expeditions into Texas. One stopped at the Nueces River and the other two briefly took over San Antonio.

Fearing capture of the government, President Houston ordered the Congress to meet in Houston, but the citizens of Austin resisted and the governmental papers, at least, remained in Austin. On the last raid, the Mexican soldiers took 67 prisoners with them back across the border and Houston ordered Alexander Somervell, a military veteran and politician, to pursue the raiders with Texas troops.

Somervell reached the Rio Grande, captured the border towns of Laredo and Guerrero, and stopped. He did not have enough supplies to plunge into Mexico, and he ordered the men to go home.

Some of the soldiers refused, and under the leadership of William S. Fisher, an experienced Indian fighter, they twice crossed the river. They first demanded and took food from the Mexican town of Mier. The soldiers left and then returned to fight a Mexican army that had come to defend the town. After fierce combat, the Texans surrendered. Santa Anna, who was once more in control of Mexico, ordered their execution. Governor Francisco Mexia of Coahuila refused to carry out the order and obtained a change in the sentence. Instead, every tenth man was to be shot. The decision about who was to die was made by having the men reach into a pot and pull out a bean. One of every ten beans in the pot was black. If the man drew a white bean, he lived. If the bean was black, he died.

William A. A. "Big Foot" Wallace, one of the prisoners, was a Scotsman who had come to Texas to avenge a relative's death at Goliad. He figured out that the black beans were larger, and after feeling around in the pot he pulled out one of the smaller white beans. The doomed men were then blindfolded and shot at dusk. Later on, some of the Mier expedition prisoners escaped, but most of them were forced to work on Mexican roads until Santa Anna freed them in 1844.

Houston also had to spend more money to suppress a feud that flared between two gangs, the Regulators and the Moderators, in East Texas. They had so terrorized Shelby County that neither the courts nor law officers could maintain order. Houston had to send soldiers to stop the fight and keep the peace. The cost and debt of government continued to mount.

President Houston and others still dreamed of Texas joining the United States. The issue became an important one in the 1844 election campaign of James K. Polk, who argued that it was the fate, or "manifest destiny," of the United States to spread from the Atlantic to the Pacific. Texas was a part of this destiny, part of the American westward movement. In February 1845, after the election of Polk, the United States offered statehood to Texas.

The Texas Congress heartily approved. The culture and customs of the people, after all, were like those of the United

States. A special convention prepared a state constitution, and Anson Jones, who had replaced Houston as president, pronounced on December 29, 1845, that "the Republic of Texas is no more." Texas thus became the 28th state of the United States, and its future was now linked with the larger future of the United States of America. Still, almost 10 years of experience as an independent republic gave Texans a pride that they have never lost.

The voters of the new state elected James P. Henderson, an attorney who had worked for annexation, as the first governor. The legislature chose Sam Houston and Thomas J. Rusk, a Nacogdoches lawyer and politician, as the first senators. Sam Houston was still at the center of Texas politics. People were either for him or against him, and the division continued as long as "Old Sam" was around.

William A. A. "Big Foot" Wallace, a survivor of the Mier expedition, figured out that the white beans were smaller than the black beans. He managed to pick out a white bean.

Thomas J. Rusk, one of the heroes of the Battle of San Jacinto. When Texas became a state in 1845, Rusk and Sam Houston were chosen by the Texas legislature to represent the state in the U.S. Senate.

The act of statehood brought the Lone Star State a burst of business growth, but also warfare. Mexico had never admitted that Texas was independent. Now that the United States had accepted Texas, there would be hard feelings and possibly war. As a precaution, President Polk sent an army led by General Zachary Taylor first to Corpus Christi and then to the north bank of the Rio Grande, across from Matamoros, to protect the new state. A Mexican army gathered on the south bank, and Mexico vowed to halt American aggression. From their viewpoint, Taylor had already trespassed on Mexican soil. Fighting broke out, and in May 1846 the United States declared war on Mexico. Taylor won two quick victories near Brownsville—the battles of Palo Alto and Resaca de la Palma.

More than 8,000 Texans joined in the fight, and Taylor found them difficult to control. After the capture of the Mexican city of Puebla, for example, the Texan soldiers paraded around the plaza on horses, mules, and donkeys. They galloped and trotted in circles, leaped on and off their animals, and picked up sticks from the ground while racing about. They wore a variety of odd clothes and hats, displayed full beards, and were covered with dust. Each was armed with a rifle and a pair of Colt revolvers. Their ruthless attitude earned them the name "Los Tejanos Sangrientes" (the bloody Texans).

Taylor's army thrust deep into Mexico, while another American army under General Winfield Scott attacked through the Mexican port at Vera Cruz. Santa Anna, Texas's old enemy, took charge in Mexico once more, but lost to both Taylor and Scott. After bloody fighting, Scott and his soldiers captured Mexico City. The killing

into what is now Wyoming. Neither the people of Santa Fe nor the U.S. Army thought that Texas had a valid claim. The question of the western boundary was finally settled by the U.S. Congress through a series of laws called the Compromise of 1850. In this legislation, Texas gave up its western claims for the present boundary with New Mexico, and in exchange for the loss in land the United States gave the state $10 million. Texas used part of the money to pay off the debts of the old Republic; the rest was spent for education, public buildings, and internal improvements, such as roads and bridges. The state also placed $2 million in an education fund to provide for public schools in the future.

Texas, meanwhile, grew in population and business began to prosper. In 1836 there were 35,000 people in Texas, in 1850 the population was 212,000, and by 1860 it was 604,000. Newcomers settled mainly in the eastern and southeastern parts of the state, where they filled in the open spaces of the pine forests and coastal prairies up to the escarpment lines of the Great Plains. There the pioneers hesitated—because on those high plains they faced unsolved problems of dry weather and Comanches.

People came to Texas to find a better life. Not only were there Anglo-Americans from the South, but also smaller numbers of Germans, Czechs, Poles, Swedes, Norwegians, Danes, French, Italians, and Irish. More than 9,000 Germans, sailing in immigrant boats from Europe, settled in a band of farms and towns, including Houston, Galveston, San Antonio, New Braunfels, Fredericksburg, and Castroville.

stopped, Santa Anna resigned, and peace negotiations resulted in the Treaty of Guadalupe Hidalgo, in which Mexico at last recognized the independence of Texas. The boundary was set at the Rio Grande. Mexico also gave to the United States the land that would become New Mexico, Arizona, and California. In return, the United States paid Mexico $15 million plus about $3 million for Mexican debts to American citizens. This payment resulted from the confused peace terms dictated by Nicholas Trist, the U.S. official in Mexico, and the reluctance of the U.S. Senate to debate the treaty.

For Texans the Treaty of Guadalupe Hidalgo settled the southern boundary, but not the border to the west. Texas claimed about half of what is now New Mexico, and a long panhandle of land that reached northward through the Rocky Mountains

General Winfield Scott led another American army to victory at Vera Cruz. He then captured Mexico City, thereby ending the war.

Migrants traveled to Texas in boats and wagons, on horseback, and on foot. They sometimes came from Louisiana and entered Texas through Nacogdoches on roads that were unpaved dirt ruts troubled with tree stumps. Such roads slowed travel to a crawl of two or three miles per hour. If the roads were wet, wagons got stuck in holes and had to be pried loose. Rivers were dangerous to cross and frequently a ferryboat had to float people, animals, and wagons from one bank to the other.

Some people traveled by stagecoach at a cost of about 10 cents per mile. That too was a rough way to go. In 1848 the Abbé Domenech, a Roman Catholic priest, trav-

eled from Houston to San Antonio by "poste," or stagecoach, an open wagon drawn by four horses. It left Houston with a gallop and clattered across a loose, seven-foot-wide plank bridge over Buffalo Bayou. On the road the wagon bounced off trees and stumps. The miserable Abbé was soaked in a rainstorm, dumped into a ravine when the driver fell asleep, and tumbled head over heels when a panther jumped upon the lead horse. It might have been safer for the Abbé to walk.

After locating a likely spot, the typical pioneer bought a farm from an empresario or a land agent. Next he had to find fresh water and build a house. Water usually

Terraqueous Machine

Long before he became famous for the invention of condensed milk, Gail Borden, Jr., lived in Galveston for 14 years. Born in New York in 1801, he traveled to Texas in 1829. He started a newspaper, became the customs agent for the Republic of Texas, surveyed the land for the city of Houston, and helped sell land for the city of Galveston.

Above all else he was an inventor, and one of his worst failures was the terraqueous machine. This was a wagon with a sail on it that could move on land or water. He tested it first with friends at midnight

on the beach but had to put on the brakes because his passengers were so frightened. The second test came in daylight, and with the wind full in his sail he headed straight into the surf. The wagon tipped over, 50 feet offshore. No one was hurt, but everyone got wet. When asked where Borden was after the accident, one of the dripping adventurers said, "Drowned, I do most sincerely hope. He richly deserves it!"

Borden did not drown and he continued to invent. He became particularly fascinated with the thought of condensa-

tion, or a chemical reaction to reduce a substance to a denser form. He tried it first on meat and made a foul-tasting meat biscuit. It was nutritious, but no one wanted to eat it. In 1856 he succeeded in condensing milk and later made a fortune with the Borden Company in Connecticut.

He died in 1874 but left an interesting thought for lovers. Joe B. Frantz, his biographer, quoted Borden: "The world is changing in the direction of condensing.... Even lovers write no poetry, nor any other stuff and nonsense, now. They condense all they have to say, into a kiss."

Gail Borden, Jr.

These German settlers, attracted by the prospect of cheap land, are on their way to New Braunfels by wagon train in 1845. The abundance of land also attracted immigrants from Ireland, Italy, Sweden, Norway, and Poland.

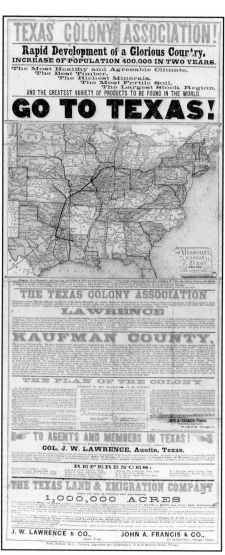

Posters such as this one, which appeared in New Orleans in 1836, lured hundreds of thousands of settlers to Texas. In 1836 the population of Texas stood at 35,000 people. By 1860 it was 604,000.

came from springs, or from a creek or river. Later the farmer might dig a shallow well and catch rainwater off the roof of his cabin. The water was held in a cistern, a large tank made of wood or stone, or in barrels. Pioneers then made crude wooden cabins by cutting trees, chopping off the branches, and laying the logs across one another to form a square. These first cabins were small, without windows or floor, and the bark was left on the trees. When they had time, the settlers made better log houses with the bark stripped away and the corners neatly notched so that the logs interlocked. The gaps between the logs were chinked, or filled, with mud, rocks, and small pieces of wood. Such houses were still usually one room but often had a floor, windows, door, and fireplace.

Inside the house were pegs and shelves for storing clothing and food. Furniture was homemade—usually a table and chairs. Beds were wooden frames with rope or rawhide lacing. On top was a mattress made of grass,

corn husks, or Spanish moss stuffed inside a large sack. Often there was a spinning wheel to make thread and yarn, and a bucket to carry water. There were dishes to eat from, and gourds to drink from. There was often a rough plank floor and a sleeping loft on the rafters for children. Greased paper was used to cover the windows; glass was too expensive and hard to transport.

To enlarge their homes, people often built a second house and connected it to the first one with a roof. They left a walkway, called a dog trot, through the middle to help keep the rooms cool. The log house and cabin were built everywhere in Texas where trees were available, and they became symbolic of frontier life, just as the tepee was a symbol of Indian life. Eventually, after people built new houses out of lumber or brick, their old log house was used as a building for farm equipment.

The next task after building a cabin and assuring a water supply was to clear land for planting. This meant burning the grass off the prairie, or cutting trees and pulling stumps in wooded areas. Once there was a clear spot, the pioneer turned the sod with a wooden plow tipped with iron and pulled by mules, horses, or oxen. It was a point of pride and skill to be able to plow a straight furrow, and to do this people frequently looked over their shoulders to see if the line was accurate. When Anson Jones was president of the Republic, a toast, or salute, at a dinner for him read, "His Excellency the President, Anson Jones. Chief plough-man in the cornfield, he turns his furrows handsomely, and never looks back." This was considered a high compliment.

The farmers in north and central Texas planted the prepared soil with corn or wheat. They also raised livestock, mainly cattle. In the south and east the farmers grew cotton. Most farms had a milk cow, some chickens, maybe a pig, sheep, and fruit trees, and a small garden for vegetables, all for home use. If they produced success-fully the farmers traded their corn, livestock, and cotton in the nearest town.

Everyone worked. Children could do farm chores from a young age, six years old or so. They fed chickens and pulled weeds out of the gardens, while older children milked cows, took care of herds, chopped wood, and helped in the fields. Women and girls worked around the house cooking, making clothes, washing, taking care of the garden, spinning, hauling water, and mind-ing the babies. Men and boys worked in the fields, hunted and fished for food, skinned wild game, cut trees, cleared land, dug wells, and took care of the work animals.

There was no electricity. People worked during daylight, sunup to sundown. It was expensive to burn candles, so after dark families relaxed and taught the children by the light of the fireplace, or went to bed.

A typical meal on the frontier would be roasted meat, corn bread, and black coffee. A Mexican family might make tortillas or tamales from the corn. When available, pecans, peas, apples, honey, turnips, and sweet potatoes would be added to the diet. Most early settlers wore buckskin (smooth

Louis Hoppe fecit.

YENBERG'S, *FARM*, Bluff · William
La Grange, Fayette County, State of TEXAS

animal hide) clothes. These clothes were tough, homemade, and uncomfortable in hot weather. In the 1830s settlers gladly gave them up as more cotton cloth became available through the town merchants. People also made cotton or flaxen cloth at home and colored it with the juice of berries or bark. On their heads women wore bonnets, and men hats made from beaver skin, buckskin, or straw.

Farming was hard work, so Southerners often brought slaves with them. It became illegal in the United States and Texas in the early 19th century to import slaves, but they could still be bought and sold within the country. At the time of the Texas Revolution about one-seventh of the population was African-American; by 1860 this figure had increased to one-third.

Slaves lived much the same as their owners. They ate the same sorts of food and lived in cabins near the owner's house. They spent most of their time working in the fields. Usually, they had Sunday and a

German-born artist Louis Hoppe painted the farm of Julius Meyenberg, another German immigrant, around 1864. More than 9,000 German immigrants settled in Texas towns such as New Braunfels, Castroville, Galveston, and San Antonio.

A former slave works at a spinning wheel. Emancipation day for the slaves in Texas occurred on June 19, 1865. Since then, June 19, known as Juneteenth, has been celebrated throughout the state.

Cynthia Ann Parker, shown here with her daughter Prairie Flower, was kidnapped by Comanches in 1836 and adopted by a Comanche family. She took a Comanche name and married a chief. In 1860 she was captured by Texas Rangers and removed from her Comanche life. Unhappy, she starved herself to death.

half-day Saturday off. Then they took care of their own houses and gardens. They usually received new clothing twice a year and were taken care of by the master when they were sick. Slaves, however, received almost no education or training in special skills such as carpentry. They could not marry, travel, or earn money for themselves without permission from their master. In addition, slaves always lived with the threat of being beaten or sold to someone who would separate them from friends and family. The numerous examples of slaves who tried to escape to Mexico, and freedom, testify to the essential unhappiness of their condition.

Before the Civil War, nine out of ten Texans lived in the country and made their living by farming. There were country churches, stores, and trading posts, and peddlers to help them, but because of time, distance, and slow travel people found it difficult to get together. When they did gather for celebrations and house building it was a memorable affair, and people concentrated months of socializing into a single evening. Noah Smithwick described a wedding among the young people of Austin's colony. After the ceremony and a supper, the room of the house was cleared for dancing. To the music of a fiddle, they did stomping, hopping dances called "double shuffle" and "cut the pigeon's wing." The floor was made of rough, heavy unfinished planks. Splinters could drive through the soft sole of a moccasin, so people exchanged shoes and took turns on the planks. Smithwick said, "We just literally kicked every splinter off that floor before morning."

Although most people lived in the countryside, it was the towns that had the newspapers, theaters, schools, courthouses, stores, and churches. Into the towns came items that farmers could not make for themselves, such as gunpowder, needles, nails, coffee, medicines, guns, books, and boots. From these same places were sent the products of the countryside, such as cotton, cattle, skins, pecans, and corn. Towns like Galveston, which began as a port in 1838, Dallas, which started as a trading post in 1842, and Fort Worth, which grew up around an army post in 1849, were important as distribution points.

So was Houston, a town started by Augustus C. Allen and his brother John K. Allen in 1836 and named for their friend Sam Houston. It was the first capital of the Texas Republic and located not very far from the battlefield of San Jacinto. Houston was a rowdy place, as were most early Texas towns. Francis Lubbock, who lived there in its early years, told this story about an uncle of Charles Hedenberg, a Houston merchant: The uncle had decided to move permanently to Texas and arrived by steamboat. He placed his trunk at the Hedenberg store and walked out to see the town. In a short time he heard gunshots and saw a clerk from the Texas Congress carried off to a doctor. As he passed the Round Tent Saloon he heard more shots and a wounded soldier almost fell on him. In front of another saloon a man banged out the door with a large stomach wound from a Bowie knife. The uncle hurried back to the Hedenberg store. "Charley," he said, "I have seen enough. I wish to return home

immediately. I do not wish to see any more of Texas." With that announcement, he left, never to return.

Because the roads were so bad and transportation so important, townspeople tried to figure out ways for the farmers to move about more easily. The towns paid to smooth the roads, build bridges, and pull tree stumps, but the most important development was the construction of railroads. This began in 1853 with the Buffalo Bayou, Brazos and Colorado Railway. Businessmen built it to encourage planters of the Brazos River area to ship their cotton over the railroad to Buffalo Bayou, and from there by small steamship to Galveston. At that port the cotton bales could be transferred to oceangoing ships and taken to markets in Europe.

After this first success, railroads began to appear in east and southeast Texas, centered mainly in Houston. In 1860 a cannon boom announced the first train from Houston to Galveston. The rails of the Galveston, Houston and Henderson Railroad reached 50 miles across the land to a two-mile trestle spanning the water to the Island City.

With better transportation, the state became more accessible to outsiders and grew in population. As a result, the frontier pushed westward into Comanche territory. To protect settlers, in 1849 the U.S. War Department built a string of forts some 350 miles from Eagle Pass on the Rio Grande to Fort Worth west of Dallas. In 1852 the War Department moved the line 100 miles farther west, and built a second line of forts between the Rio Concho and the Rio Grande. In spite of these lines, the Comanches raided past the forts into settled areas.

Since the time of the Austin settlement, Texans also relied upon "Rangers," state deputies recruited for temporary service, to fight outlaws and Indians. In the 1840s the Texas Rangers popularized the Colt revolver as an ideal weapon for a person on horseback. Single-shot rifles were impossible to reload from a galloping horse, but the new revolver could fire five times (later six), and then be used as a club in close combat. The utility of the gun was recognized nationally during the Mexican War of 1846–1848.

Galveston began as a port in 1838. Its bustling harbor (top) played an important role in the growth of the Texan economy. Carl G. von Iwonski's painting, Theatre at Old Casino Club in San Antonio, *indicates the role of the growing cities as cultural centers.*

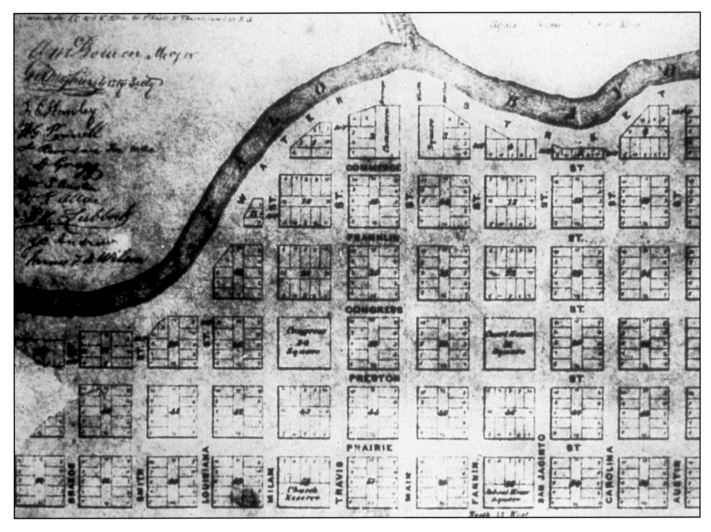

The original street plan of the city of Houston, founded in 1836 by Augustus Allen and his brother John.

During the Indian conflicts before the Civil War, at the Battle of Pease River in 1860, Texas Rangers captured Cynthia Ann Parker and her 18-month old daughter, Prairie Flower. Cynthia Ann, now called Naduah, had been kidnapped by Comanches when they raided Parker's Fort 24 years earlier. She had been adopted by an Indian family, grown up as a Comanche, married Chief Peta Nocona, and had borne three children. Naduah had forgotten the English language and looked like an Indian, except for her light skin and blue eyes. When she first heard her old name, she burst into tears—and that was how the Rangers discovered who she was.

The Texas legislature gave Naduah money and land on which to live, but she nevertheless tried to return to the prairie to find her Indian husband. She failed, and in 1864, after the death of her daughter, Cynthia Ann Parker starved herself to death.

Her husband never remarried and died of an infected wound. Her son Pecos died of disease. Her remaining child, Quanah Parker, however, lived to be the last of the great Comanche war chiefs.

In 1859 the Texas legislature banished all remaining Indians to the Washita River area of Oklahoma. The exceptions were the peaceful Alabama-Coushattas in East Texas and the Tiguas at El Paso. This officially ended most Indian life in Texas, but raids by Comanches and Kiowas continued into the 1870s and fighting with the Apaches extended into the 1880s.

Texas, meanwhile, faced another serious conflict. During the 1850s the United States split over the question of slavery. Abolitionists, who wanted to abolish slavery, had worked for 30 years to end it, and the successful election of Abraham Lincoln to the Presidency in 1860 was the turning point in their struggle. Lincoln was

a member of the Republican party, which hoped to stop the spread of slavery. Lincoln's victory triggered the secession movement, the action of southern states to leave the Union.

Although most Texans had voted for Lincoln's opponent, John C. Breckinridge of Kentucky, they now had to decide to join or reject the South. Sam Houston was governor at the time and wanted to give Lincoln a chance. He bravely asked a hostile crowd, "Will you now reject these last counsels of your political father and squander your political patrimony in riotous adventure, which I now tell you . . . will land you in fire and rivers of blood?" No one listened. Texas joined the Confederate States of America in February 1861 and prepared for war.

Most white male Texans eagerly greeted the opening events of the Civil War. They rushed to join military units, while the

women began to make flags, tents, uniforms, and other war equipment. About 60,000 men eventually went to war. This was two-thirds of the white male population between the ages of 18 and 45, and it meant that the war was important to almost every family. No one remained untouched by the conflict, which explains why so many people remembered the war long after it was over.

Texan soldiers fought not only at Glorieta Pass in New Mexico, Galveston, and Sabine Pass, but also traveled eastward to fight with various Confederate armies. Albert Sidney Johnston, for example, one of the best Texan generals, died at the Battle of Shiloh in Tennessee. The most famous unit, however, was Hood's Texas Brigade. Formed in 1861, it was led by Brigadier General John Bell Hood of Kentucky, who adopted the Texan soldiers as his own. The brigade served mainly in the

The first railroad in Texas, the Buffalo Bayou, Brazos and Colorado Railway, began in 1853. Railroads quickly spread throughout Texas. Shown here is an early train and its crew.

In July 1861, at the start of the Civil War, U.S. ships set up a blockade off the port of Galveston. The blockade cut off just about all of the traffic going into and out of the port. On January 1, 1863, the Confederate forces struck back, bombing the Union ships and driving them out of Galveston.

East with Robert E. Lee and fought in at least 24 battles. At one time it had 4,500 men, but the heavy wounds of war reduced it to only 617 men. Southern generals praised its bravery and the men sang this song as they marched:

> There's a yellow rose in Texas,
>   That I am goin' to see.
> No other soldier knows her,
>   No soldier, only me.
> She cried so when I left her,
>   It like to broke my heart.
> And if I ever find her,
>   We never more will part.

Eventually, the blockade of the Confederate coastline by Northern ships and the defeat of Robert E. Lee ended the Civil War in 1865. Texans fought the last battle of the war at Palmito Ranch near Brownsville, where 30 Northern soldiers died needlessly. The war had already ended, but the Texas force under Rip Ford found out only from the prisoners they had captured. On June 5 the United States flag flew again over the courthouse at Galveston. General Gordon Granger announced at the island port on June 19, 1865, that the slaves were officially free and that the war was over.

Carl G. von Iwonski's 1862 painting The Terry Rangers. *The Eighth Texas Cavalry, also known as the Terry Rangers, saw extensive action during the Civil War. The man in the center, waving his canteen, is Sam Maverick, who joined the Rangers in 1862 at the age of 25. When he died at the age of 98, he was the last survivor of the Terry Rangers.*

At this time the state was in chaos. The Confederate States of America (C.S.A.) had gone out of existence and there were no courts, law officers, or postal system. Confederate money was worthless, and Southern soldiers on their way home with almost nothing after four years of fighting looted the storehouses and property of the C.S.A. Major H. A. Wallace, for example, heard about the end of the war while he was on board a C.S.A. steamship. Major Wallace simply claimed the vessel as his own and used it to set up a freight business between Houston and Galveston.

Young black people, free for the first time, took to the roads and walked to the towns, with the mistaken idea that the U.S. Army would take care of them and that life was better in the cities. Railroads were in poor condition and everything had stopped. People wandered the streets, waiting. As a newsman observed, "Business is at a standstill. The machinery is out of gear, and every one appears to be waiting for the crack of the whip which is to start us—God knows where."

It was the U.S. army of occupation that got things going again by providing a

The Battle of Palmito Ranch was fought after the Civil War had officially ended. But the Texas force under Rip Ford did not know about the war's end until their Northern prisoners told them.

structure for the operation of business and society. The officers bought supplies for the troops from local merchants, appointed people to run local governments, and made certain that African Americans were treated fairly. This Reconstruction period was complicated by an epidemic of yellow fever that struck Galveston, the headquarters for the army, in 1867.

Yellow fever, or yellow jack, as it was sometimes called, was a highly contagious disease passed from one person to another by mosquitoes. Symptoms included fever, red eyes, headaches, and "black vomit" caused by internal bleeding. About one-fourth of the people infected died, but if victims survived they possessed lifelong immunity. Port cities of the Gulf of

Mexico were particularly vulnerable because the disease was often carried by travelers. Yellow fever struck Texas in 1839, 1844, 1847, 1853, 1859, 1864, 1867, 1870, and 1873. The epidemic was particularly severe in 1867 because of the large number of Northern soldiers who possessed no immunity to the disease. It spread along 200 miles of coastline and penetrated 125 miles inland. At the time no one knew what caused yellow fever, but they did know that the epidemic would end with the first hard frost.

In Galveston in 1867 three-fourths of the population caught the disease and people died at a rate of 20 per day. A worker at the military barracks observed: "Every morning when the sun rose and the roll was called

In 1866 voters elected James W. Throckmorton, a former Confederate general, as governor. "Old Leathercoat," as he was called, was removed from office the following year by U.S. General Philip Sheridan, the military supervisor of Texas during Reconstruction.

many familiar faces had disappeared forever. Merry, laughing and buoyant with life and spirits in the evening, silent and stiff in the arms of death in the morning.... Disease lurked in the sands, in the water, in the wind.... It was a dreadful summer."

Thinking it might help, people burned buckets of tar in the streets. They used ice to ease the fever and volunteer nurses tended the dying. The epidemic did not end until November when the weather cooled, killing the mosquitoes that spread the disease. But by then, most people had caught the fever and had either died or had survived and gained immunity.

When yellow fever returned to Galveston in 1870, widespread panic seized the coastal towns. Armed men from Houston stopped a trainload of fleeing people and turned it back. With shotguns, Houston enforced a quarantine against the Island City and threatened to tear up the railroad track. The isolation of Galveston helped to prevent the spread of the deadly virus. Another epidemic broke out in 1873. Then, in 1876, the state used quarantining against New Orleans when yellow fever appeared there. This technique of isolation kept the disease under control until science discovered a better way to fight it in the early 20th century.

Through this hardship Texas politicians tried to meet the requirements necessary to reenter the Union. Voters selected James W. Throckmorton, a former Confederate general, as governor and, as the United

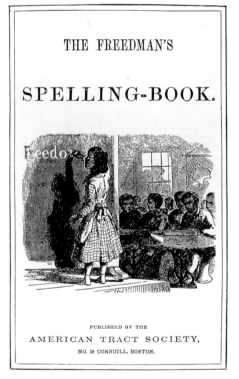

THE FREEDMAN'S

SPELLING-BOOK.

PUBLISHED BY THE
AMERICAN TRACT SOCIETY,
NO. 28 CORNHILL, BOSTON.

The Freedmen's Bureau established more than 100 schools throughout Texas, providing ex-slaves with both teachers and books like this one.

States required, approved a new constitution that abolished slavery. African Americans were not given the right to vote, however, and their activities were regulated by "black codes." These were laws that required blacks to have jobs and to be obedient and respectful.

In addition, an illegal, secret organization, the Ku Klux Klan, flourished from 1866 to 1899 throughout much of the South and Texas. Klan members, who wore white sheets and pillow cases with eye holes to disguise themselves, used threats, assault, and murder to suppress black voting and social ambitions. Klan activities were widely reported in East Texas, but seem to have disappeared after 1869. At that point the founder of the Klan, Nathan B. Forrest of Tennessee, thought that it had gotten out of hand and disbanded the organization.

U.S. congressmen objected to such action in Texas and other southern states because they thought that blacks were not being given true equality. As a result, Congress divided the South into military districts and required that the Reconstruction work be done again under military supervision.

In Texas, General Philip Sheridan removed Governor Throckmorton and appointed Elisha M. Pease, a former Texas governor who had opposed secession. The new governor had little power, however, and was more of a caretaker. The army protected blacks and gave emergency food to needy people. Many of the relief activities were carried out by the Freedmen's Bureau, directed by the army, which operated in Texas from late in 1865 until 1868. The bureau worked throughout the South, but its greatest accomplishment in Texas was setting up more than 100 schools for African Americans.

One of the more interesting workers for the bureau was George T. Ruby, a free African American born in New York City in 1841. He was well educated and became a correspondent for a Boston newpaper, *The Pine and Palm,* during the Civil War. In 1864 he began working for the education of blacks in Louisiana. In 1866 he traveled to Texas to continue his educational work as a teacher and traveling agent for the Freedmen's Bureau and in the meantime became a state senator from Galveston. Ruby helped to organize the Republican party in Texas and participated in the constitutional convention of 1869. He returned to Louisiana in 1873 after the Republican party lost control in Texas to edit a New Orleans newspaper. Ruby left behind, however, an example of a capable, educated black man at a time when many white people doubted such achievement was possible.

In November 1869, Texas voters approved of a new constitution written by a

special convention and elected as governor Edmund J. Davis, a Republican candidate supported by the U.S. military. Davis had been in Texas since 1838 but had fought for the North during the Civil War. The new legislature confirmed the 14th and 15th Amendments to the U.S. Constitution, as it was required to do. These amendments protected the civil rights of African Americans: the 14th defined citizenship to include blacks, and the 15th made clear that they had the right to vote. As a result, in March 1870 President Ulysses S. Grant declared Reconstruction in Texas at an end.

With military occupation ended and the new constitution in place, most rebels could vote again. They moved quickly to regain lost power, and in the election of 1872 voters selected a legislature of Democrats. The lawmakers acted swiftly to limit Davis's power, and the governor found himself fighting what he called a "slow civil war" of bitter words and criticism. In 1873 Richard Coke, a former Confederate army officer, defeated Davis for the 1874 term. Davis blocked the first floor of the capitol and asked President Grant for help, while Coke and his men took over the second floor. Both sides were armed to the teeth, and a small civil war between the floors of the capitol seemed imminent. When Grant sent a telegram refusing help, Davis gave up—to the cheers of a statewide celebration. In Galveston, for example, the local artillery company hauled its cannon to the beach and fired 100 times for this "triumph of the people."

The new governor and legislature moved rapidly to clear away any remnants of Reconstruction. They fired Republicans from public office, cut government expenses, and called for yet another convention to rewrite the constitution. The new 1876 state constitution was long and complex. It cut the governor's term to two years, limited state debt, allowed land grants for railroads, gave land for schools but cut tax support to operate them, provided a bill of rights, and increased the number of state officials to be elected by the people, rather than appointed by the governor. The convention also confirmed the right to vote regardless of race, but ignored a petition to grant voting rights to women.

In February 1876 the voters approved the new constitution, the same basic document that now rules Texas. It has been amended through the years more than 300 times and is like a patchwork quilt. The many changes reflect the restless spirit of a state that is searching for equality and justice for all citizens.

Black teachers worked to establish schools for themselves and their children after the Civil War. By the end of the 19th century, the literacy rate for blacks was 60 percent, a remarkable accomplishment for a people who were purposely kept from reading before 1865.

Frank Collison, a cowboy, on his horse. He has all the equipment of a typical cowboy: broad-brimmed hat, neckerchief, gun, high-horned saddle, lariat, and of course, a horse.

Chapter Four
The Last Frontier

After the interruption of the Civil War, people began to migrate once more to the Lone Star State. In the 1870s the population almost doubled, and growth continued at that pace for the rest of the century. By 1900 Texas was the sixth-largest state in population, with more than 3 million people. Available land was still the main attraction of Texas. The legislature gave away 32 million acres for railroads and sold nearby land for as little as $1.50 per acre. Until 1899 a family could claim 160 acres free as a homestead. All they had to do was live there for three years. A single person could do the same and get 80 acres. In Texas, land was still a bargain.

There was little thought, however, about the rights of Indians. While the Civil War continued and the men were absent, the frontier line was weak. Indians out of Mexico and the Great Plains, mainly Comanches, Kiowas, and Apaches, raided and burned the ranches and farms. Settlers pulled back, gathered together for protection—"forted up" as it was called—and waited for the war to end.

After 1865, U.S. soldiers took up fighting the Indians of the West. At first they could not match the hit-and-run tactics of the Indian nomads. From the backs of galloping horses, the Indians could use their bows fast enough to keep an arrow flying in the air at all times. The arrows hit with enough force to drive the shaft through a buffalo or man. The soldiers, often on foot, at first fought back with single-shot, muzzle-loading rifles. They were not successful, however, until they used cavalry to attack and destroy the supplies and equipment of their enemy.

The Indians pillaged almost as they wished. They killed about 100 settlers a year, and the Texans begged for help. Not much happened until 1871, when General William Tecumseh Sherman visited Texas. He was the commanding officer of the United States Army and he knew about the ways of marauders. During the Civil War, he had led an army across Georgia that looted and burned its way to the sea.

Sherman doubted that the Texas situation was as bad as he had heard until he visited Fort Richardson, the most northern of the Texas line of outposts. While he was there a wounded man staggered in to report an Indian raid at Salt Creek. The Indians

The war was relentless. The horse soldiers chased the tribes to the reservations and even entered the grounds to arrest renegades, who periodically left the reservations to make raids. The soldiers followed the Apaches across the deserts of West Texas into the mountains and crossed the Rio Grande to fight the Kickapoos in Mexico. They burned villages found outside the reservations, captured and then killed Indian ponies, destroyed food supplies, and killed Indians whenever possible. Between 1865 and 1881, there were 846 army–Indian clashes in the West; 61 soldiers won the Medal of Honor, the highest recognition for bravery awarded by the United States.

The turning point of the Indian wars came in Texas, at Adobe Walls. Buffalo hunters had moved into the Texas Panhandle in 1874, settling near the ruins of an earlier trading post. In June of that same year about 250 Cheyenne, Comanche, and Kiowa Indians attacked the 28 men and one woman of the camp. The hunters held off the attackers, who were led by Lone Wolf and Quanah Parker, the son of Cynthia Ann Parker, with their powerful breech-loading buffalo guns. Such weapons were loaded from the same end of the barrel as the trigger. They were much faster to use than muzzle-loaders, which were loaded from the end of the barrel. On the second day of the fight, Billy Dixon, a buffalo hunter, knocked an Indian off his horse 1,500 yards away. That was a remarkable shot, almost one mile in distance. After five days the Indians retreated, leaving four white people dead at the post.

In retaliation, the U.S. Army sent out

Quanah Parker was the last of the great Comanche war chiefs. He was relentlessly pursued by the U.S. cavalry before he surrendered in June 1875. Until his death in 1911 he served as a spokesman for the Plains Indians living in Oklahoma.

had captured a small wagon train, stolen the mules, burned the vehicles, and killed seven men. They had scalped one man, cut out his tongue, and left him tied to a wheel with his face in a fire.

Sherman learned that this same Indian band of Kiowas and Comanches had come close to killing him as he rode to Fort Richardson with a small escort. That did it. The general angrily unleashed the cavalry against the Indians to drive them permanently onto the Indian reservations in Oklahoma established in the 1830s.

3,000 men from different directions to find the Indians' secret winter camps in the Cap Rock region of the plains. The scouts of Colonel Ranald Mackenzie discovered five villages hidden in Palo Duro Canyon. Quietly, at dawn, Mackenzie led his troopers and their horses down the steep trails into the canyon. Then, with a surprise attack, the soldiers stampeded the Indian horse herd and charged the tepees.

The Comanches and other Indians scrambled up the canyon walls to escape. All but four survived the assault, but they left behind their horses and winter supplies. Mackenzie ordered his men to burn their flour, blankets, smoked meat, new repeating rifles, ammunition, and tepees. A few years earlier he had captured some Indian horses, but Quanah Parker had stolen them back again. This time Mackenzie ordered the Indian herd of more than 1,000 horses taken to a nearby canyon and shot.

It was brutal, but that was a way to win. The Comanches were left on foot in the winter with no supplies. Meanwhile, on the reservations, the U.S. government cut food rations to the Indians in half so that the

famished tribes would have to eat their horses, their source of transportation. There would be no more horses for Quanah Parker. At the same time, Mackenzie and others continued their pursuit, and in June 1875, after a winter of hunger, Parker surrendered and agreed to live on a reservation in Oklahoma.

In the far southwest corner of the state, troops, including the famous black "buffalo soldiers," chased down the last of the Apaches. These black U.S. soldiers had earned their nickname from Indians in Kansas, who had learned to respect their fighting ability. Included in the army forces, moreover, was Lieutenant Henry O. Flipper, the first African American to graduate from the U.S. Military Academy. In a joint U.S.–Mexican campaign from 1878 to 1881, Mexican soldiers defeated the Indians led by the Apache chief Victorio, while in the Diablo Mountains of West Texas other Apache bands found only death and defeat by U.S. soldiers. These encounters ended all Indian warfare in Texas.

The Native Americans thus vanished from Texas. Only the two small reserva-

This thatched-roof porch in front of a tent was part of a fort built by the U.S. government to protect white settlers from Indian raids. The white picket fence gracing the front provides a homey touch.

General William T. Sherman, the commanding officer of the U.S. Army that drove the Indians off the Great Plains. In his memoirs he wrote, "War is cruelty, and you cannot refine it."

These soldiers were members of the U.S. Army's 10th cavalry, an all-black unit. The Indians called them "buffalo soldiers" and greatly respected their fighting ability.

and a buffalo hunter might kill 250 per day. Sir St. George Gore, an Irish "sportsman" who toured the West in the 1850s, had his servants hand him loaded guns so that he did not have to reload, just to see how many he could kill in one day. He shot 1,000.

The hunters stripped off the buffalo hide and cut out the tongue, a delicacy, leaving the carcass to rot. By 1878 they destroyed the vast southern herd that roamed into Texas and by 1884 the northern herd that reached into Canada. About 100 million buffalo lived on the Great Plains in 1840, but by 1887 only a little more than 1,000 remained. The Texas legislature voiced some concern about the approaching extinction of the buffalo, but General Sherman explained that it was necessary to destroy the Indians' food supply. With the herds gone, the Indians were dependent upon the reservations for food and would stay in Oklahoma. It also meant that the prairies were empty, ready for use by ranchers.

The Spanish had begun the range-cattle industry in the brush country south of San Antonio and along the Rio Grande, but it declined in the 1700s. Anglo-Americans revived it, however, in the early 1800s. James Taylor White, who became one of the earliest ranchers in southeastern Texas, gathered wild longhorn cattle in 1819 to sell in New Orleans. Richard King purchased 75,000 acres of cattle range in South Texas in 1852. With his partner Mifflin Kenedy, he expanded the King Ranch and made it famous; over time it became one of the largest in the world.

Longhorns were plentiful and cheap, even free if you could catch them. About 5 million mavericks roamed the prairies of

Hunters skin a buffalo in 1874. In 1840 there were about 100 million buffalo living on the Great Plains. By 1887 only a little more than 1,000 remained.

tions, the Tigua and the Alabama-Coushattas, remain in the state as a reminder of the people who were there to help Cabeza de Vaca and his lost men on a cold November day on the beach at Galveston Island. The Plains Indians lost not only because of the U.S. Army but also through the bloody work of the buffalo hunters. Bison hides sold for $3.75 in the 1870s and hunters like Billy Dixon at Adobe Walls ventured forth to make their fortunes. Buffalo were unafraid of gunfire and thus very easy to kill. Using a Sharp's rifle, which hurled a heavy bullet, hunters could calmly stand in the midst of a herd without moving position and shoot. The record for a single stand was 90 animals,

South Texas. The name *maverick* comes from Sam Maverick, a Texas politician and rancher who at the time of the Civil War allowed his cattle to wander about without brands.

Before the war there had been a few cattle drives to various places, but afterward the growing population of the East and North provided a market for beef and leather. Chicago slaughterhouses, where cattle were prepared for market, paid $40 a head, while longhorns in Texas brought $4. It took about $1 each to drive them along a trail to a railroad. Thus there were high profits to be made at a time when Texas was hobbled by the hard times of Reconstruction. This simple economic situation inspired

the long drive and the cattle bonanza, a great source of wealth.

In the spring and summer of 1866 cowboys drove 260,000 head to Sedalia, Missouri, over a trail that cut through settled country. Farmers complained of trampled crops and the Texas tick fever that infected their cows. The angry settlers then patrolled their land with shotguns to turn away approaching herds. Joseph G. McCoy, a cattle buyer, solved this hostile standoff. He took over a remote prairie village and turned it into a cattle town, equipped with hotels, saloons, barns, and pens. McCoy persuaded the Hannibal and St. Joe Railroad to build tracks to his village, which gave him a link to the Chicago stockyards.

He then marked the Chisholm Trail, the first of the great cattle trails, west of the settlements to his town of Abilene, Kansas. About 35,000 longhorns arrived in 1867. Over the next 20 years Texas cowboys drove 6 million longhorns to Abilene and other Kansas cattle towns.

Trail driving became a profession. Contractors supplied manpower and equipment to drive the herd, which allowed owners to stay at home and care for their ranches. The drovers, or cowboys, tended to be young men, although a few women were known to have driven cattle. For example, Lizzie Williams, a rancher from Austin, drove a herd to Kansas in the 1880s. She rode in a buggy and had her cowboys lay a rope

Longhorns

The Spanish brought cattle to the New World beginning with Columbus's second voyage in 1493. As they took both horses and cattle with them to missions and settlements, some animals escaped and others were turned loose. Breeds intermixed and the multicolored longhorn evolved into a superb open-range cow. Herds were running wild from the Red River to the Rio Grande by the time Stephen F. Austin reached Texas in the 1820s.

The longhorn was thin and flat sided. Its

horns stretched as wide as eight feet from point to point and caused the animal to wobble when it walked, but the tough longhorn could take care of itself on the range. It would protect its young from wolves, go for days without water, eat prickly pear cactus during drought, and withstand both heat and cold.

The main drawback of the longhorn was that there was too much bone and horn and not much meat. As better beef cattle came to Texas and the West in the late 19th century, the longhorn almost disappeared. In

1927 the U.S. Forest Service collected a small herd in Oklahoma to preserve the breed. In Texas, Sid Richardson, a Fort Worth millionaire, and J. Frank Dobie, a writer, rounded up another herd in 1948 and placed it at Fort Griffin State Park near Albany.

The idea of burning the hide of an animal to identify the owner is age-old; the Spanish brought the idea to the New World. It came to Texas as early as 1762, and in 1848 Texas provided for the registration of brands. Often they are modified letters. A lean-

The Texas longhorn is today a popular symbol throughout Texas—providing the nickname for the University of Texas's athletic teams.

ing letter is "tumbling." A letter on its side is "lazy." Short, curved strokes at the top make it "flying" or "running." The famous brand of the King Ranch is a running W. A part

circle at the bottom makes it "rocking." There are also bars, chains, stripes, and slashes. The purpose is to make the brand different so that it is easy to recognize and hard to change.

A herd of cattle crossing the Rio Grande from Mexico. The growing U.S. population after the Civil War led to an increased demand for beef.

This hat rack was made from the horns of Texas longhorn, which were in demand for a style of furniture that became popular, along with cowboy literature, in the last part of the 19th century.

around it at night to keep out rattlesnakes. (According to traditional wisdom, a rattlesnake will not crawl over a rope.) The cowboys faced the dangers of Indians, bandits, blizzards, stampedes, dust storms, and drowning at river crossings. They sometimes worked 36 hours straight for $15 to $20 per month plus food. It was hard work. Teddy Blue, a cowboy who wrote a memoir called *We Pointed Them North*, said:

> But when you add it all up, I believe the worst hardship we had on the trail was loss of sleep. There was never enough sleep. Our day wouldn't end till about nine o'clock, when we grazed the herd onto the bed ground. And after that every man in the outfit except the boss and the horse wrangler and cook would have to stand two hour's night guard. Suppose my guard was twelve to two. I would stake my night horse, unroll my bed, pull off my boots, and crawl in at nine, and get about three hours' sleep, and then ride two hours. Then I would come off guard and get to sleep another hour and a half, till the cook yelled, "Roll out," at half past three. So I would get maybe five hours' sleep when the weather was nice and everything smooth and pretty, with cowboys singing under the stars. If it wasn't so nice, you'd be lucky to sleep an hour. But the wagon rolled on in the morning just the same.

The trail boss picked the route and made work assignments. A chuck wagon with a cook and supplies traveled along and the men ate meals of beans, cornbread, molasses, coffee, beef, and wild game. The cowboys took along a remuda, or herd, of saddle horses. The men worked more hours than the horses and so would change mounts during the day. It took about a dozen men to handle 3,000 longhorns. The cattle would eat grass along the trail, but if grass or water were scarce, herds could starve or go blind from thirst.

The early ranchers usually bought or claimed land along streams and took over surrounding land even though they did not own it. When the state offered the land for sale, they bought as much as they could and then rented the rest. In such manner the ranchers spread through West Texas.

In 1876, two years after the defeat of the Comanches, Charles and Mollie Goodnight established a ranch in Palo Duro Canyon. With a partner, Goodnight took over a million acres and handled 100,000 head of cattle. He helped to populate the northern plains with longhorns by finding a trail northward. Mollie was the first Anglo-American woman on the plains and she helped the cowboys with her home medicines. She used coal oil on lice, prickly pears on wounds, and buffalo meat broth as a

A dozen cowboys could handle about 3,000 long-horns. In addition to the herd of cattle, they also took with them a herd of spare horses and a chuck wagon stocked with enough food to last a month on the trail.

tonic. She was shocked at the widespread killing of the buffalo and persuaded her husband to save a few calves to preserve a small herd.

During the depression of the 1870s, when prices for cattle were low, the ranchers just left them on the prairie. The tough range cows scratched through the winter snow to eat the dry, nutritious grass underneath. Half the cattle driven northward were used to put stock in the empty spaces of Colorado, Wyoming, Montana, and the Dakotas. After a while there were too many cows for the land to feed. This situation caused trouble later, but for the moment the cattle business brought money to Texas and helped the state recover from the Civil War.

This episode in Texas history created one of the finest frontier types, the cowboy. Often the subject of art, stories, music, and movies, cowboys lived a life of danger and adventure. They also got involved in gunfights. At Old Tascosa in 1880, for instance, Sheriff Cape Willingham banned guns within the city limits in an attempt to tame the town of its wild manners and prevent killings. Fred Leigh, the foreman of a nearby ranch, refused to give up his gun. The sheriff met him as he dismounted in front of a saloon, asked for the pistol, and raised a blunt shotgun to enforce the request. In reply, Leigh leaped back on his horse and closed his hand around his six-shooter. Sheriff Willingham blew him out of the saddle with a shotgun blast. Leigh became the second man to be buried in Tascosa's Boot Hill Graveyard.

For some unknown reason the sheepherder never became a popular figure like

the cowboy. Some people today go around trying to look like cowboys, but no one tries to look like a sheepherder. Yet the life of a shepherd was just as dangerous and lonely. He had to spend months by himself looking after flocks of very stupid animals and protecting them from mountain lions and wolves.

The sheep and goat industry came along at the same time as the cattle business, and some of the ranchers, including Richard King, kept sheep as well as cattle on their land. In the town of Kerrville, Charles Schreiner made sheep raising popular on the Edwards Plateau. He was a former Texas Ranger and cattleman who became a merchant and banker. When people borrowed money from him, he made certain that the borrower used half the money to raise sheep. Schreiner also knew the great value of mohair, or goat hair, and saw the possibility of mixing goats and sheep on the same range. Kerrville thus became a mohair market for the United States, and even today the Edwards Plateau produces most of the mohair in the nation.

Once in a while the sheep and cattle people clashed because the animals and methods of work were so different. The nearly wild cattle needed long grass to eat, plenty of water, and a rider on horseback to keep up with them. The passive sheep, by

In 1876, after the Indians had been driven out of Texas and into Oklahoma, Charles and Mollie Goodnight established the first cattle ranch in the Texas Panhandle.

Cattle were not the only animals raised in 19th-century Texas. Sheep and goats were also big business. At left is a group of Mexican sheepshearers near Fort McKavett in 1892. Below is a vast herd of goats in the Davis Mountains.

contrast, fed on short grass and found enough water in the morning dew. Flocks required a herder on foot, sometimes with a dog, to look after them. The cowboys, who thought that anyone on foot was something less than a man, made fun of the shepherds and raced their horses through the frightened flocks. There was also an ethnic difference. Cowboys were usually Anglo-Americans; shepherds were often Hispanic. The basic arguments, however, centered upon the use of pastures, water, and fences. These rights, however, were most seriously challenged by the farmers who came to the prairies to tame the open expanses.

An early visitor to Lubbock, in West Texas, observed, "What a clean stretch of land. Why I could start a plow point into the soil and turn a furrow two hundred miles long without a break." By 1890 the first farmers were wrestling with the two

major problems of the plains—lack of water and lack of trees. American pioneers were used to having plenty of rain and wood. The rainfall was necessary to raise crops of corn and cotton, and the timber was necessary for building houses, barns, and fences. The Great Plains offered very few of these essential items. That is why the prairies of the country were the last parts to be settled; farmers did not know how to deal with the dry, barren grasslands.

Early West Texas settlers grubbed in the ground for roots to burn and hauled in water in barrels. A young housewife who had spilled a bucket of water while climbing down from a water wagon said, "Oh God, how I hate a country where you have to climb for water and dig for wood." The plains farmers built their first houses out of sod. They constructed walls and roofs from large rectangles of grass, roots, and dirt cut

from the prairie, and sometimes pulled apart wagons to provide wood for framing in doors, windows, and roofs. The sod house was cool in the summer and warm in the winter. It was fireproof and lasted about six years. If it rained, however, it turned into mud and might wash away. It also attracted unpleasant visitors—snakes and rodents—that crawled in and out of the walls.

The first farmers cleared away a circle of brush around their houses to protect against grass fires. From a distance the area looked like a large nest with the sod house in the middle. That is why cowboys called the farmers "nesters." Because there was almost no firewood, the farmers burned hay, cornstalks, roots, sunflower stalks, buffalo dung, and cow chips (dung). Buffalo and cow droppings, surprisingly, produce a slow, smoldering fire. The odor was not very pleasant, but the fire it produced was better than nothing on a cold day, and a passing trail herd might well leave behind enough fuel for the winter.

Blizzards, dry spells, grass fires, and grasshoppers caused other hardships for the settlers. In 1874 millions of grasshoppers devoured the grass and everything else down to the bare ground in a large swath from the Dakotas to Texas. This sort of disaster occurred regularly. The grasshoppers would descend in great, whirring, dark clouds on the fields. Farm families frantically fought back with brooms, fire, and even chickens. It usually was of no use, and in just a few hours the work of the season would be lost. Wheat and corn would be eaten to the last shred, and the insects even gnawed on fences and wooden tool handles.

Then the grasshoppers would fly on. Nothing really stopped them until the invention of pesticides in the mid-20th century.

One of the most important pieces of equipment for the prairie farmer was the windmill. The nesters needed water for family and livestock, and windmill companies provided a machine to solve the problem. Interestingly, underneath the dry grassland were aquifers, or subsurface water reservoirs. Workmen would first pound a pipe several hundred feet into the ground, like a metal straw, to the water level. On top of the pipe, workers would then put together a large fan mounted on a wooden frame. The fan turned in the wind and provided power to run a pump that sucked the water to the surface. The farmer or rancher then collected the water in a large tank or barrel and saved it for later use.

The large, 14-foot-diameter fans of the famous Eclipse windmills, factory-made in Beloit, Wisconsin, rested on squat towers. They turned their faces into the wind and became defiant symbols of hope in a forbidding land. They were the landmarks of settlement on the barren horizons. As cowboy James Stallings explained, "There were no roads, no towns for miles and miles. You moved from windmill to windmill, and you got your directions from windmill to windmill."

With the occupation of the land, farmers and ranchers wanted to fence in their property. No one had enough wood for use on fences, but everyone, it seemed, had the same idea about what to do—build a fence out of wire. It would be cheap and easy to put up, and if there were barbs on it the cattle would leave it alone. The difficulty

was to figure out what kind of barbs to use and how to keep them in place on the wire.

The problem was solved in 1874 by Joseph F. Glidden. He was an Illinois farmer who invented a double-strand wire with a short, sharp barb wrapped through it. This was the answer for fencing in a treeless country. Glidden began producing the wire and sold it widely in Texas by 1876. Farmers and ranchers thus closed in thousands of acres of land in the next decades, but that too created some difficulties.

In 1879, for example, rancher Charles Goodnight rescued a small band of peaceful Pueblo Indians from some anxious travelers who mistook them for fierce Comanches. The Pueblos had gone to trade with the Kiowas and tried to take a shortcut back to New Mexico. Goodnight said to the chief, "You surely know the way back to Taos. Haven't you lived in this country all your life?" The chief answered in frustration, "Alambre! Alambre! Alambre! Todos partes." ("Wire! Wire! Wire! Everywhere.")

The large ranchers stretched the barbed wire fences across their pastures. The huge XIT Ranch in the Panhandle strung 6,000 miles of barbed wire over the landscape. The nesters fenced off their grain fields and people tended to cut one another off. Fences sometimes blocked roads, hindered access to schools and churches, and blocked postal delivery. Ranchers fenced in public land and sometimes boxed in another ranch or

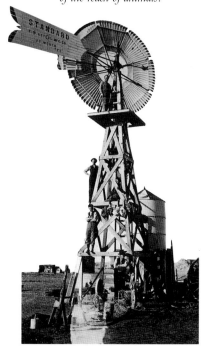

Thorny Fence

From the moment they arrived in Texas, settlers tried to fence their land. People used rocks, rails, briars, cactus, and smooth wire, but nothing worked well in the dry land of grass and longhorns. "Thorny fence," as it was first named, appeared in 1867, and thereafter some 1,600 different types of barbed wire were developed. Joseph F. Glidden of Illinois, however, made a double-strand wire with barbs that became the most popular.

At first Texas ranchers were doubtful that it would work, but John W. Gates, who sold the wire for Glidden, built a corral in downtown San Antonio. He bragged, "The cattle ain't born that can get through it. Bring on your most ferocious steers, gentlemen, and see how this barbed wire corral will hold them."

The local ranchers herded in 25 mean longhorns and waited. The steers charged the fence just once and then retreated to the center of the corral to bellow in protest. Gates was right. Glidden sold 5 tons of wire in Texas in 1874, 40,000 tons in 1880, and 200,000 tons in 1900.

Barbed wire proved to be an ideal solution for fencing in the vast open spaces of Texas. More than 1,600 different types of barbed wire were invented.

farm. Sheep could not get through to fresh pasture and cattle could not get through to water. As a result, everyone cut the fences and trespassed. In rebellion against the barbed wire enclosures, secret groups calling themselves Owls, Javelinas, and Blue Devils went out at night to cut any fences they could find. They threatened people who put up barbed wire and they burned pastures. Three people died in this range war and damage was placed at $20 million.

Governor John Ireland called a special session of the legislature early in 1884. The lawmakers made it a felony to cut a fence, and a minor crime to put up an illegal fence. The legislature said that ranchers who built a fence across a public road had to put in gates every three miles and keep them in good repair. Texas Rangers were assigned to catch the criminals, and the fencing war stopped.

The fencing of the Great Plains also created a situation that led to a major disaster. Throughout the West, severe winters from 1885 to 1887 killed thousands of cattle. It is estimated that on the southern ranges of the West about 85 percent of the herds died from freezing and starvation. Range cows, like longhorns, survive a blizzard by drifting along with their tails to the wind and snow. This time, the storm-driven animals walked up to the barbed wire fences, stopped, ate the remaining grass, waited, and died. There was no food for them and nowhere to go. The bodies stacked up and other cows walked up the bodies and over the fences to the next barbed line, then froze to death.

The great "die-up," as it was called, took the heart out of the cattle bonanza. People

The Texas Rangers

The term "ranger" was used in Texas within two years of the first Anglo-American settlements in 1821. It refers to a special state law officer who was called when a problem was bigger than the local people could handle, yet too small to require an army. In early days Rangers rode against Indians and border bandits. In later times they were used against outlaws, rustlers, fence-cutters, rioters, and striking workers.

The most lasting legend of the Texas Rangers involves a worried Dallas mayor who asked for help to stop an illegal prizefight. When the nervous mayor met the train to pick up the rangers, only one man stepped off. The mayor asked why there weren't more men and Ranger Bill McDonald replied, "Hell, ain't I enough? There's only one prize-fight." McDonald then took care of the problem. This resulted in the myth of "one riot, one Ranger."

These Texas Rangers, members of Company B, pose with their rifles in 1900.

with money decided to invest it elsewhere. The cattle trails closed and there were no more long drives. The Indians lived on reservations and cowboys became ranch hands. There was no more free land; by 1890 the Texas frontier was gone.

Farming changed as the frontier vanished and railroads gave access to cities. People could make money with crops produced for a market, and farmers began to use more machines to help them in the fields. In 1870 farmers planted 1 million acres of corn, the leading crop, all by hand. In 1900, with the help of machines, the farmers planted 5 million acres. The production of other grains, such as oats, sorghum, wheat, and rice, followed a similar pattern. The most important Texas crop, however, was cotton.

After 1880 Texas led all other states in cotton production. As cotton gins, compresses, and cottonseed-oil mills followed the railroads, cotton growing and marketing employed more people than any other industry. The farmers planted early in the spring and started picking in July to avoid the damage caused by the boll weevil. This was an insect pest that migrated from Mexico in 1892. The weevil deposited eggs in the cotton boll, the pod of the cotton plant that contains the seeds, and the young insects

destroyed the fiber. Farmers discovered that cotton grown at higher altitudes avoided the pest. This encouraged the growing of cotton on the Great Plains once a technology of irrigation developed.

Machines for planting cotton, cutting stalks, and cultivation came into use in the 1880s, but harvesting was done by hand until the 1950s. It was back-breaking work, often done by black families. The pickers would drag 8-foot sacks to hold the cotton pulled from the bolls. The sacks held 25 pounds of cotton and a good worker could fill 10 sacks per day.

The plants grew only about 20 inches high, which meant that people had to bend over to pick. After several hours the workers got backaches, and some tried crawling on their knees. The only relief came at lunchtime or when the sack was full. It was then carried to the cotton wagon, weighed, and dumped. The work left white salt lines from sweat on the workers' shirts and blouses, but it was hardest on their hands.

A retired engineer in Beaumont who had experienced such labor recalled:

> You got up in the dark, ate your breakfast and got to the field by daylight. The cotton could be wet with a chilly dew, which could wet your clothes, but worst of all it softened

Cotton became big business in late 19th-century Texas. At top, planters with wagonloads of raw cotton line up at the Austin Gin and Manufacturing Company. The Southern Pacific rail yard in Houston (center) and the port of Galveston (bottom) were important hubs for the transportation of cotton to the rest of the United States and Europe.

revolving wires, or teeth, the gin machinery separated the seed from the entwined fiber by pulling the fiber through narrow grates that left the seeds behind. Some of the cotton seed was kept for the planting of future crops; the rest was crushed to make cottonseed oil, a product used in food and soap. The cottonseed hull was used for animal feed and fertilizer. The most valuable part, the fiber, was pressed and tied into rectangular bales weighing about 500 pounds. Railroads used a compress to squeeze the bales in order to reduce their size so that more could be carried on a rail car. At the ports, for shipment overseas, dock workers used special screw jacks that compressed the bales even more to allow a ship to carry more bales. At their destination, often the textile mills of England or Scotland, the cotton was unloaded, cleaned, spun into yarn and thread, and made into cloth, which was then sold throughout the world.

This shift to cash crops meant that Texas farmers were now dependent on the whims of distant markets and business changes elsewhere in the country or the world. Before the Civil War the richest people in Texas were the planters, but afterward their place was taken by merchants and bankers in the cities. The farmers felt sharply this loss of prestige and influence. They tried to organize themselves to regain political power, but in the long run nothing helped. They did find a champion, however, in Governor James S. Hogg, who was elected in 1890. In particular, he wanted railroads to charge fair rates for cotton shipments, and he helped create the Texas Railroad Commission, which had the power to

your fingers so the sharp point on the cotton burrs pricked your fingers until they might bleed, but you kept on picking. In a little while the sun would come up and drive the dew away. Then the burr points would get sharper, but you kept on picking.

From the fields the loose cotton was taken by wagon to a gin, usually located on the plantation or in a nearby town. With

The Hoggs of Texas

After Brigadier General Joseph Lewis Hogg died fighting for the South in 1862 and his wife died the next year, their son James Stephen was left to run the family plantation. The family estate was gradually sold to pay for the education of James and his four siblings, and he became a lawyer, newspaperman, and politician. He served as an attorney for Wood County in 1878, as a Texas district attorney from 1880 to 1884, and as Texas attorney general in 1886. In 1890 he was elected the first governor born in the Lone Star State.

In fiery speeches to eager crowds, James Hogg praised simple country virtues of honesty and hard work and blasted the undue power of large capitalists, insurance companies, and railroads. Working into a sweat in the hot, humid Texas climate, Governor Hogg would fling off his coat, drop his suspenders from his shoulders, gulp large swallows of water from a bucket, and splash his forehead. He spoke to his audience with earthy language, but when ladies were present the most derogatory phrase he would use was "by gatlings."

During his terms in office, from 1891 to 1895, Hogg championed the small farmers by pushing for laws to regulate railroad rates and land speculators. For this work he became known as the "people's governor," but he left office in debt and returned to private legal practice determined to rebuild his fortune. Through legal work, real estate purchases, and oil investments in Austin and Houston, he died a rich man in 1906.

Hogg and his wife, Sarah, had four children—Will, Ima, Mike, and Tom. His daughter was named for a charac-ter in a poem, *The Fate of Marvin,* written by his brother, Thomas E. Hogg. Contrary to popular jokes there were no children named Ura, Heza, and Sheza, but Hogg somewhat embodied the image of his name, since he was 6 feet 3 inches tall and weighed between 250 and 275 pounds, one of Texas's largest governors. Will and Mike Hogg became noted for the development of a wealthy Houston suburb called River Oaks and, with the other members of the family, donated their lives and fortunes to philanthropy. "Miss Ima," as she became af-

Governor James S. Hogg, known as the "people's governor," was the first governor of Texas to be born there.

fectionately known throughout Texas, helped to start the Houston Symphony Orchestra in 1913 and led in the cultural development of Houston until her death in 1975.

---

supervise railroad charges. In 1897 the chairman of the commission claimed that lower rates had saved farmers $800,000.

In spite of the rural past, the future of Texas was to be found in the cities. Important in the 19th century for urban centers was the building of an infrastructure—telephones, telegraphs, railroads, schools, water supplies, paved streets, sewers, hospitals, police and fire departments, market places, electric power systems, and city government—the facilities and organizations that helped a city operate. In particular, the latter part of the 19th century was a time of massive railroad building that linked the farmers to the cities, and one city to another.

At the time of the Civil War, Houston was the railway center of Texas, with lines that stretched 50 to 100 miles in five directions. After the war the railroads revived and began building once more. The Texas government encouraged them by granting them large chunks of land, which the railroad companies would then sell to pay for the cost of construction. In 1870 Texas had 583 miles of track, in 1900 it possessed

10,000 miles, and by 1905 the Lone Star State had almost 12,000 miles, more trackage than any other state in the country.

The railroads built their lines from several directions. Following early wagon routes, local companies laid track from the Gulf Coast northward. National railroad companies competing to construct transcontinental lines built across Texas from east to west and from west to east. These national companies were a part of the effort to construct transcontinental lines from the Atlantic to the Pacific. An important moment for Texas came when the Houston and Texas Central Railway from the south connected with the Missouri, Kansas and Texas Railroad from the east at Denison in 1873. Three years later, when the width of the rails was changed to a standard gauge, or distance apart, a boxcar could roll all the way from New York City to Galveston with no difficulty. A spiderweb of railroads soon covered the state as trains appeared in Austin in 1871, San Antonio in 1877, Abilene in 1880, and Amarillo in 1887.

Among other things, the railroads transported lumber to the West. Lumberjacks

entered the East Texas pine forest in 1870 to cut and float logs down the Sabine and Neches rivers to sawmills at Orange and Beaumont. The logs were sawed into planks and shipped to the treeless places of the West so that people could live in houses of wood rather than homes made of sod and dirt.

John Henry Kirby's lumber company in Houston became the first multimillion-dollar business in Texas. At its peak in the early 1900s it employed 16,500 people. Some folks said that the sun did not rise in East Texas until John Kirby rolled over in bed, stretched, and opened his eyes in the morning. During the 1920s, unfortunately, the industry declined due to overcutting. It did not recover until a second growth of trees came of age 25 years later.

Texans both loved and hated their railroads. Immigrants used them to move westward, and the railway lines encouraged settlement so that they could sell the land given them by the state. Farmers and ranchers used the railroads to send their cattle and cotton to market and to receive supplies. The train became a symbol of modernity,

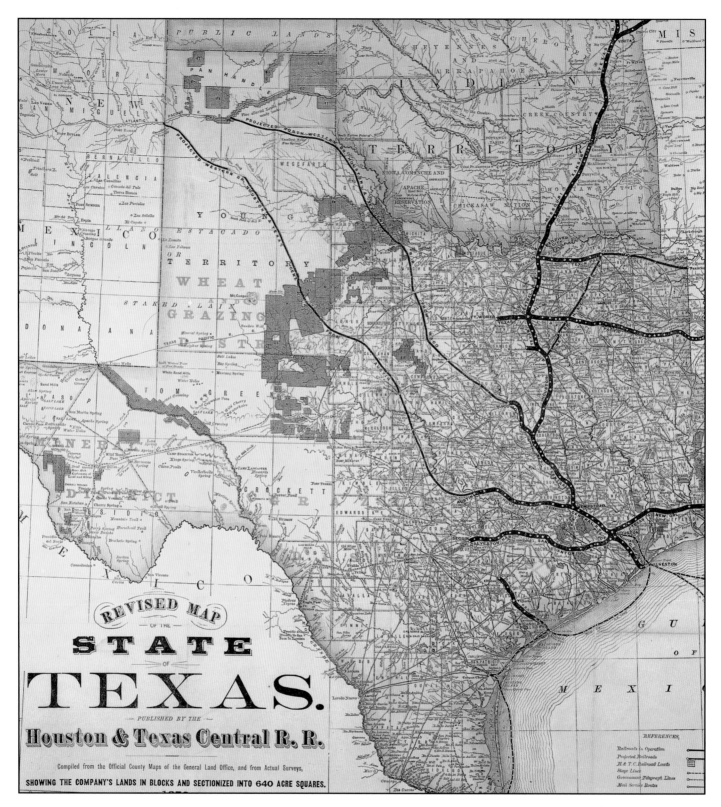

REVISED MAP
OF THE
STATE
OF
TEXAS.
PUBLISHED BY THE
Houston & Texas Central R. R.

Compiled from the Official County Maps of the General Land Office, and from Actual Surveys,
SHOWING THE COMPANY'S LANDS IN BLOCKS AND SECTIONIZED INTO 640 ACRE SQUARES.

The Houston & Texas Central Railroad published this map of Texas in 1876. The thick black lines represent railroads that were in operation at the time.

and towns would pay to have the trains chug with all their noise and smoke right down the main street. When times were hard, however, the railroads became a target for people's anger. People nicknamed the Houston East and West Texas Railway (HE & WT) "Hell Either Way Taken." They called the International and Great Northern (I & GN) "Insignificant and Good for Nothing." Texans complained about railroad abuses, and at the same time wanted more railways.

The trains were important for communication, since they carried passengers as well as freight. As people traveled, they spread news and ideas. Equally important

for this spread of information were the telegraph and telephone lines. In 1854 the Texas and Red River Telegraph Company strung wires through treetops into East Texas and brought instant news to businessmen and newspapers. For instance, it carried the notice of the election of Abraham Lincoln, the news that triggered the Civil War.

Another company, the Texas and New Orleans Telegraph Company, strung wires between San Antonio, Austin, New Orleans, and Galveston. It began service in 1866 and by 1870 there were 1,500 miles of live telegraph wire in Texas. The telegraph connected the frontier forts and marched on poles westward beside the railroads. Newspaper articles often carried the note, "By telegraphic intelligence," which meant that the information came over the telegraph lines. Texas was thus able to tap into the thought of the world.

Telegraphs, however, required the use of skilled operators who knew Morse code, a system of dots and dashes. That was not necessary with another major communication invention, the telephone. All you had to do was talk, and Texans were good at that. In 1876 Colonel Alfred H. Belo visited the World's Fair at Philadelphia, where Alexander Graham Bell demonstrated his new device. Two years later Belo set up a telephone line, the first in Texas, between his home and newspaper office in Galveston.

Others liked the idea, and Galveston put together a telephone system in 1879. Houston installed telephones the same year, followed by Dallas and San Antonio in 1881 and Lubbock in 1902. The first connections between cities came in 1893 with

a line between Houston and Galveston; the first long-distance conversation was about the weather. When asked what it was like in Houston, the answer was, "Horrid and warm." Not much has changed; that could be true of Houston weather today. By 1900 long-distance telephone wires stretched out of Texas to St. Louis, Kansas City, and Chicago. The XIT Ranch in West Texas even used telephone lines as the top strand on its barbed wire fences. Because they were so easy to use, telephones were a great technological advance.

But communication and advancing technology required educated people. It did no good to send a message over a wire, in a letter, or through a newspaper if it could not be understood by the person at the other end. People had to be educated, and the job of education belonged to the schools and libraries.

For the most part, before the Civil War libraries and schools were owned by small groups or individuals. An exception to the private libraries was the Texas State Library, started in 1839 by the Republic of Texas. Poorly cared for, its meager contents burned in 1881 when the capitol caught fire. The library, however, revived and became important as a major reference center after 1900, when it began to receive regular funding from the state. At the same time,

Log trains in the Piney Woods of East Texas. The expanding railroad network in Texas allowed the lumber industry to fill the growing demand for lumber on the treeless plains of West Texas.

This spacious zoology laboratory at the University of Texas in Austin (top), equipped with microscopes for each student, stands in stark contrast to this public schoolhouse in Live Oak County. The quality of public schools throughout Texas varied widely in the late 19th century.

cities were aided by Andrew Carnegie, a steelmaker from Pennsylvania who educated himself by reading borrowed books. Carnegie gave considerable money to build libraries for the people throughout the country. With buildings donated by Carnegie and with the encouragement of the Texas Library Association, which was organized in 1902, most of the larger Texas cities established public libraries in the early 1900s.

Education also improved as permanent public school systems were begun during the Reconstruction period and supported by the state. The constitution of 1876, however, made local governments responsible for public education, but when this produced poor quality schools the state took over again in 1884. African Americans were taught from the start in separate classes, an extension of the segregated society that had developed as part of Southern culture. Even though their separate schools often had the worst buildings, books, and teachers, blacks cut their illiteracy rate almost in half by 1900. Still, at the end of the century, 40 percent of the blacks could not read or write.

To help people learn to farm better, the United States government helped the state establish the Texas Agricultural and Mechanical College in 1871. It opened in 1876

in a rural area of Brazos County and almost lost one of its first 40 students when a pack of wolves attacked the young man near the main school building. The state also opened the University of Texas in Austin, with a medical branch in Galveston, in 1883. Church-supported colleges appeared, including Baylor University (founded in 1845), supported by the Baptist Church in Texas; Trinity University (1869), supported by the Presbyterian Church in Texas; Add-Ran College (1873), later renamed Texas Christian University, which was started by Addison and Randolph Clark, who were Disciples of Christ ministers; and Abilene Baptist College (later Hardin-Simmons University), founded in 1891 by the Sweetwater Baptist Association. These public and private schools taught white students subjects such as mathematics, history, engineering, literature, medicine, and law. The church-related schools usually included a heavy dose of their particular religion, including daily chapel services, in their schedules.

Many of the schools, colleges, and libraries were constructed in the towns and cities, where there were concentrations of people. The towns, moreover, took pride in local colleges as a symbol of modernity and at times provided land as well as cash bonuses to attract them.

As the urban areas grew, they had to provide water, sewers, street lighting, pavement, fire departments, crime control, and transportation. The most basic need was a pure water supply, not just for drinking but for fighting fires, cleaning, and industry.

In Galveston people caught rainwater as it dripped off roofs and stored it in cisterns. To fight fires the citizens built a system of pumps and pipes to use seawater. It did not work well, and in 1885 a nighttime fire with sparks swirling in the wind burned 42 blocks of homes and offices. Looking for a better supply, the city subsequently drilled for water on the mainland and pumped it through pipes underneath the bay to the town.

In Houston both fire and disease caused a search for better water in the 1890s. The town drew its drinking water from Buffalo Bayou—which is where it also dumped its sewage from toilets and slaughterhouses. Bad odors and eels that had swum into the system came out of the water pipes. People were just beginning to understand that "germs" in the water could cause sickness, and Houstonians complained of bowel trouble. They solved their problem by drilling water wells to an aquifer and putting fresh water into their pipes. Dallas did the same thing about the same time.

Houston, however, got into additional difficulty with the sewage. Businessmen wanted the U.S. Army Corps of Engineers to deepen Buffalo Bayou so that it could be used by large ships. The engineers refused so long as the city dumped its raw sewage into the stream. The city responded between 1899 and 1902 by building one of the most advanced sewage disposal systems

in the world. It was designed by Alexander Potter, a New York engineer brought to Houston for the project. A network of sewer pipes collected the sewage from around the city and pumped it to a central station. There it flowed into a series of filters—rough stone, gravel, sand, and coke. The filtered water then flowed into the bayou. Potter insisted that the effluent, or outflow, was pure. To prove it he scooped up a glassful and drank it. He said that it tasted fine, and he did not get sick.

In the latter part of the century Texas cities also began to use garbage dumps. Previously, towns had allowed pigs to run loose to eat the garbage, but the pigs made smelly wallows in the streets and were by no means thorough in the disposal of garbage. In the late 1800s, therefore, towns began to employ garbage collectors to pick up the trash at night and haul it in wagons to dumps beyond the city limits. This was all part of an effort to clean up the streets and make them passable.

Streets in Dallas and Houston were well known for being muddy in winter and dusty in summer. People experimented with various paving materials, such as planks, bricks, gravel, wooden blocks, crushed rock, and asphalt, which seemed to last the longest. In Galveston the problem was sand, rather than dirt and mud. The city tried pavements of oyster shells and wooden blocks covered with tar. The blocks were easy on horses' hooves, and quiet compared to bricks, but they floated away in floods

Main Street in Dallas at the turn of the century. By the end of the 19th century, telegraph and telephone lines had connected Texas to St. Louis, Chicago, and Kansas City.

A San Antonio trolley car in 1904. Trolleys began appearing in the streets of some big eastern cities in the 1880s and 1890s. The San Antonio electrical trolley began operation in 1890 and replaced the mule-drawn cars that had operated since 1878.

and hard rains. Outside the cities the roads remained dirt pathways.

City people, especially in the business sections, provided sidewalks of planks or bricks. The towns were "walking cities," where traffic moved on foot, horseback, or animal-drawn wagons. After railroads came to town, it was only a short while before streetcar companies provided rail cars pulled by mules. Although it was easier for people to ride than walk, the mule cars were no faster than walking, and the mules could be a bother. In Houston, for example, a mule slipped on a curve, fell, and ended up on its back underneath the car. The driver thought it was dead until the mule kicked its way through the floor and stood up. The rest of the night was spent trying to figure out how to get the mule out of the car.

When electricity came to the towns electric trolleys replaced the mules. The trolleys were much faster and permitted the expansion of the city boundaries. People could now live in suburbs and ride the trolley to work in the downtown area. Electricity also made possible better lighting of streets at night. Previously, towns had used gas lamps, but they were both dim and expensive. In 1882 the Brush Electric Company demonstrated a string of electric lights in Galveston that made the street "light as day," according to the local newspaper. The same happened in Dallas in 1882, and two years later in Houston. In Austin, in

1894–95, the Fort Wayne Electric Company from Indiana built 31 towers. They were 165 feet high and gave Austin what was commonly called "artificial moonlight." Each tower provided a circle of blue-white light 3,000 feet across that was bright enough to allow a person to read the time on a pocket watch at midnight.

In 1870 the largest towns in Texas were Galveston (14,000 people), San Antonio (12,000), Houston (9,000), Brownsville (5,000), Austin (4,000), and Jefferson (4,000). Galveston was the state's main port, and Houston served as Galveston's doorway into the interior of Texas. San Antonio, the old capital of Spanish Texas, served as the supply place for the cattle industry. Brownsville, which had started as a fort in the war with Mexico, became an entry into Mexico. Austin was assured of a future as the state capital and site of the state university. Jefferson, however, was doomed to failure.

This East Texas town, named for Thomas Jefferson, started in 1836 on the banks of Big Cypress Creek. The creek led to nearby Caddo Lake and to the Red River. Merchants found deep water at Jefferson, and steamboats from New Orleans and St. Louis came to the Jefferson docks. In 1873, however, U.S. army engineers blew up an old log jam on the Red River that had stopped boat travel on the upper part of the river. What people in Jefferson did not realize was that it also served as a dam. When the engineers blew up the jam, the logs floated away and the land drained. The water level in Caddo Lake went down, leaving the docks at Jefferson high and dry. Jefferson never grew after this and has remained a small town to the present day.

In 1900 the largest cities in Texas were San Antonio (53,000 people), Houston (45,000), Dallas (43,000), Galveston (38,000), and Fort Worth (27,000). San Antonio continued to supply the Southwest. It developed railroads and became a military center. The U.S. Army completed the first part of Fort Sam Houston in 1879, and by 1900 it was the largest base in the nation. Teddy Roosevelt gathered his Rough Riders there in preparation for the Spanish-American War in 1898. Houston grew because of railroads and small factories. Transcontinental railroads built through Dallas and Fort Worth to open that area to settlement and Dallas shipped cotton by rail to northern and eastern cities. Fort Worth started as an army post in 1849 and then became a shipping point for cattle. It became the first Texas cow town.

Galveston, meanwhile, had slipped. It was still the leading cotton shipping port in the nation in 1900, aided by harbor improvement. Army engineers scooped the bottom of the port to make it deeper. To keep the harbor clean of sand, they built two jetties, or stone walls, in the water to direct the current of the bay. In September 1900, however, the Island City suffered the worst natural disaster in the history of Texas and the United States. A hurricane struck the island and flooded the entire town. Six thousand people died. Following this event the citizens put their money and energy into building protection from the sea, and not on the oil bonanza that swept the state. Galveston thus missed sharing in the activities that helped build other Texas towns and remained a medium-sized city.

By the end of the 19th century almost one out of five Texans lived in the cities, and urban growth was faster than that of the total Texas population. All over the United States, people were moving from the country to the towns. Texas followed the same path as the other states, but a little more slowly. The future was to be found in the cities. As the anthropologist Margaret Mead explained,

> The city is a center where, any day in any year, there may be a fresh encounter with a new talent, a keen mind or a gifted specialist—this is essential to the life of a country. To play this role in our lives a city must have a soul—a university, a great art or music school, a cathedral or a great mosque or temple, a great laboratory or scientific center, as well as the libraries and museums and galleries that bring past and present together. A city must be a place where groups of women and men are seeking and developing the highest things they know.

A devastating hurricane struck Galveston in 1900, killing more than 6,000 people and destroying about one-third of the city.

The discovery of vast pockets of oil in the early part of the 20th century attracted thousands of men to Texas who hoped to strike it rich.

Chapter Five

The Development of Modern Texas

Major events in the first 50 years of the 20th century—the discovery of oil, the Great Depression, World War II—transformed the people of the Lone Star State. Yet the most significant aspect of Texas society in this period was the enduring separation of black and white people, a segregation that had been a part of Texas culture from the beginning of Anglo-American settlement. The Civil War had freed the slaves and provided equal treatment in the courts, yet the races remained separated. Black and white children did not go to school together, nor did their families go to the same churches. Whites and blacks lived in separate parts of cities and shopped at different stores. Blacks were forced to ride in separate railroad cars and could sit only in separate places set aside for them in theaters, usually in the balcony. Separate waiting rooms at the train stations, and even two sets of drinking fountains, one for whites and another for blacks, were customary in Texas during the early 20th century.

Segregation was enforced by local rules called "Jim Crow" laws, a name that came from a black theater character of the 19th century. Most importantly, however, the separation was supported by the U.S. Supreme Court's decision in the 1896 case of *Plessy* v. *Ferguson*. The justices ruled that separation of races in public facilities was legal if those facilities were the same for each. For example, a school for black children had to have desks, books, teachers, blackboards, and restrooms of equal quality to those given white children. This idea was called the "separate but equal" doctrine.

In most situations, however, blacks were assigned to the oldest schools, the most dilapidated railroad cars, and the least attractive sections of town. Even in the countryside, most African Americans made their living as poor farmworkers and lived in rented tenant houses. The memory of slavery was still there. Hispanics were not much better off, although the prejudice against blacks was somewhat worse. Since the whites held the majority of votes in elections, however, there was not much these minorities could do about their condition.

Of course, some individuals managed to succeed despite the prevailing attitudes.

Boxer Jack Johnson of Galveston won the world championship in 1908.

The Texas League of Professional Baseball Clubs was formed in 1887 with six teams. This game took place in Houston around 1890.

ing on a field near the Ursuline Convent in Galveston, introduced baseball to Texas. Young men in Galveston who had come to watch formed their own team and challenged other groups, including those in Houston, as enthusiasm for the game spread.

Professional baseball started in Cincinnati in 1869, and in 1887 four professional teams, including the St. Louis Browns and New York Giants, came through Texas showing off their skills in games against local pickup teams. Late that year the Texas League of Professional Baseball Clubs was organized in Austin. In the first season of this minor league, Austin, Dallas, Fort Worth, Galveston, Houston, and San Antonio fielded teams. Before the end of the season, so many quit (for a variety of reasons) that the league collapsed, but it reorganized the next year and kept playing. There have been many changes in teams and rules, but the Texas League still operates today.

A particularly hot rivalry resulted between the Houston Mud Cats and the Galveston Sand Crabs. At a game in Houston in 1889 the Sand Crabs led 9 to 4 in the fifth inning. In the eighth inning the Mud Cats pulled within one run. Then, with an hour of sunlight left, the umpire halted the game because of darkness. The crowd shouted "Mob him!" and chased the umpire into a dressing room. It was said that the umpire had bet money on the Galveston team and did not want to lose. He could be heard crying inside the room even with the crowd howling outside. A Houston lawyer finally persuaded the fans to go home and the umpire escaped unharmed.

Jack Johnson, for example, grew up on the rough docks of Galveston and learned to make money by fighting other black children for the nickels and dimes they received from onlookers. He made his living as a boxer, traveled far for prizefights, and won the world championship in 1908. Johnson bought fancy clothes and fast cars and taunted his opponents in the ring. White people in Texas and elsewhere in the nation resented his success and looked for a "great white hope" to beat him. That finally happened in 1915, but the fact that Jack Johnson, a black man, was a superb boxer could not be changed.

Although people read about boxing in the newspapers, the most popular sport played by Texans was baseball. During Reconstruction, Northern soldiers, play-

The baseball term "Texas Leaguer" refers to a ball hit just over the reach of infielders and too short for outfielders to catch. Such a hit is usually good enough to get the batter on base. According to a longtime Houston baseball fan, Harry M. Johnston, a young man named Ollie Pickering arrived in the city on a boxcar in 1888. He tried out for the Houston team and played the same afternoon. Pickering hit the ball seven times for seven times at bat. Each one was a quick pop just over the infield that dropped in front of the outfielders. This was the start of the term "Texas Leaguer," which came to be used by baseball commentators nationwide.

John McCloskey (center), the founder of the Texas League, was the manager of the Austin team.

Football appeared about 1890. The sport came to Texas from the East Coast, where it had evolved from a combination of soccer and rugby. Ball High School of Galveston played the Santa Fe Rugbys from the mainland in one of the early games in 1892. The Ball fans invented a cheer set to music, one of the earliest in the state: "Brekekekex, coax, coax. Bredededex, coax, coax. Ball High School! Ball High School! Yellow and blue, rah! rah! rah! Boom!!!" The Rugbys listened in amazement to the fans from the island and then trounced Ball High 14 to 0. These teams were all white; blacks had separate schools with their own teams.

Galveston, with its railroad connections, gradually began to develop as a major vacation place for Texans. The beach had always been popular. People had often used the Gulf shore for swimming, driving horses and carriages for pleasure, and gathering seashells. Bathing suits were not much available in the 19th century, so people went into the surf with their clothes on, and sometimes with them off. The city passed a law in 1877 that said swimmers had to be covered from neck to knee. Boys still often swam naked. When they were discovered, the police simply picked up their clothes and took them to the police station. The boys then had to get home as best they could.

Businessmen built bathhouses on the beach in the 1880s so that people could change their clothes and rent bathing costumes. A distant portion of the beach was reserved for blacks, who had their own bathhouse. Segregation was observed on the beach and in the surf as well. The first building to have electric lights in Texas was

a two-story entertainment center built on the beach by the streetcar company in 1881. In this pavilion the owners put a roller-skating rink and once held a greased pig scramble. A small pig with an oiled tail was chased around the rink by a large, yelling group of boys. They were supposed to pick up the pig by the tail and put him in a barrel. No one was able to do it. The contest ended with tired boys and a pig with a sore tail.

Entertainment in Galveston and other cities included circuses, tight-rope walkers, balloon launches, horse racing, fishing, bicycle riding, theaters, and local bands to play music. Automobiles, bought at first for the amusement of wealthy people and the amazement of others, began to show up on Texas streets about 1902. Small movie theaters began to appear around 1907 and radio stations by 1922. Christmas and July 4th were the principal holidays. On the Fourth there were community picnics, with patriotic speeches, barbecued beef, fried chicken, lemonade, watermelon, and fireworks. Bands played and people danced.

Turn-of-the-century bathing beauties enjoy a day at the Galveston beach. The police were unable to enforce the city law requiring a costume to cover the body from neck to knee. Here, the bathing suit is already at mid-thigh.

hang stockings by the fireplace on Christmas Eve and in the morning they would find them stuffed with fruit, candy, and toys. On Christmas day, families—parents, aunts, uncles, children—would gather for a large dinner of chicken, turkey, ham, bread, pie, and cake. The family would go to church sometime during the holiday to hear the Christmas story told once more by their church leaders.

Texas culture was also influenced by various groups seeking the inspiration of great thoughts and literature. Most of the larger cities had from an early time formed debating clubs that formally discussed various questions. For instance, in 1839 one club in Houston debated the question "Can the treatment of the Indians by our ancestors be justified?" Houston citizens also formed a lyceum in 1854 that sponsored lectures, debates, musical programs, and a free library for its members. The Houston Lyceum endured and became the local promoter for a free public library in Houston in the early 20th century, coinciding with the work of the Carnegie Foundation and the Texas Library Association.

The oldest statewide intellectual organization is the Philosophical Society of Texas, founded in 1837 in Houston by 26 political and business leaders to collect and diffuse information "which our new and rising republic unfolds to the philosopher, the scholar, and men of the world." The society met during terms of the Texas Congress but lapsed after Texas became a state in 1845. The Philosophical Society, however, was revived in 1935 as a nonprofit educational organization for Texas cultural leaders, and it continues to the present time.

Theater marquees line this Dallas street in 1922.

This was a time when ethnic groups—Czechs, Poles, Swedes, Germans, Mexicans—showed off their traditional dances and foods. It was a time for all Americans.

Since most Texans were of the Christian religion, Christmas was also important as a time of family celebration. Children would

The Members and Founders of San Antonio Chinese School 1928

關安   伍明洋   李朝

伍鴻龍   劉璠頤

伍魁煒   伍明聲   劉文晃

CROWN ART
PHOTO CO.

The Texas State Historical Association, another educational organization that continues today, began in 1897 with a meeting of interested people at the state capitol building. It started a scholarly publication, now called the *Southwestern Historical Quarterly*, that has had the longest lifespan of any intellectual journal in the state. Throughout the 20th century the association has sponsored annual meetings, books, and research about the history of the Lone Star State.

Cultural appreciation can also be seen in the examples of art and architecture that emerged from Texas society. Elisabet Ney, for instance, brought her skill to Texas from Germany in 1872 and became the state's best sculptor. She lived for a while on a cotton plantation in Waller County and then moved to Austin. For the Chicago Columbian Exposition in 1893 she carved white marble statues of Stephen F. Austin and Sam Houston. These statues now stand in the capitols at Austin and Washington, D.C. Her most notable piece is probably the marble grave covering of Confederate general Albert Sidney Johnston, in the state cemetery.

Buildings and human-made structures are often a reflection of a society's culture. "Old Red" at the Texas Medical School and the "Bishop's Palace" in Galveston are samples of the work of Texas's foremost architect in the late 19th century, Nicholas Clayton. In Waco people have preserved a graceful suspension bridge that borrowed the technology of the famous Brooklyn Bridge of New York City, then under construction. The Waco bridge, completed 13 years earlier than the larger bridge in

Brooklyn, was used to move cattle across the Brazos River in 1870. It thus brought money and importance to this previously small village.

The most important piece of architecture of the late 19th century, however, was the new capitol in Austin, built as a symbol of governmental virtue and power. Fire had

German-born sculptor Elisabet Ney at work on a bust of William Jennings Bryan. Although Ney delighted in shocking people with her curious ways, she is recognized as one of Texas's best artists.

The Rainmaker of Post City

Charles Post, the founder of General Foods. After retiring from General Foods, he built a working-person's community, Post City, in West Texas in 1906.

Charles William Post, a real estate broker from Fort Worth, invented an instant drink called Postum. This was a substitute coffee made with hot water and a powder inspired by Texas housewives who made a "coffee" from chicory and roasted wheat. Postum used the same ingredients. It gave C. W. Post his first success, and with the proceeds he began to produce breakfast cereals such as Grape Nuts at his cereal company in Battle Creek,

Michigan. Post amassed a fortune and retired in 1902. He used his money and energy to build a working persons' town, a place where in 1906 a person without much money could buy a ready-made house on a small lot at Post City. Located near the cap rock in West Texas, the town gained only moderate success in attracting residents, but Post ordered an unusual series of experiments at the town to see if he could make it rain by setting off explosions.

Post had read that it often rained after great battles in which cannons were used, so from 1910 to 1914 he ordered his workers to create "rain battles." They set off explosions of dynamite from the ground and also from kites, but the results were not considered of much significance. Today there exists no scientific evidence to support his theory. Yet, strangely, in 1913, after 13 battles with the clouds, it rained seven times.

destroyed the old capitol in 1881, and the legislature offered 3 million acres of land in the Panhandle to anyone who would build a new one. An investment group from Chicago led by Mattheas Schnell accepted the offer and Elijah Myers from Detroit drew up plans for a building similar to but a little bit bigger than the capitol in Washington, D.C.

In 1888 the handsome new capitol, built of Texas red granite, was finished. At the top of the dome stood a golden Goddess of Liberty. The Chicago investors took the land and started the famous XIT Ranch, which covered parts of 10 counties. The idea was to use the grassland for cattle and then gradually sell it off to farmers. The owners began selling land in 1901 and closed out the last of its cattle in 1912.

More important for the economy, however, was the discovery of oil—perhaps the single most important historical development in 20th-century Texas history. During past eras when the earth was forming, the sea advanced and retreated at least nine times over Texas. Deep layers of sand, gravel, and trapped plants covered the bottom of the sea. The weight of the rocks and small one-celled organisms called bacteria eating the buried plants created pockets of petroleum (oil) and natural gas and sheets of coal.

In Southeast Texas, around Houston, huge plugs of rock salt punched upward, cracking through the underground layers of sedimentary rock. Along the sides of these salt domes into the shattered rock seeped oil and gas. Sulphur deposits also came from this era of the earth's formation. These natural resources—salt, gas, oil,

The Waco suspension bridge was used to move cattle and people over the Brazos River.

and sulphur—became the building blocks of a new petrochemical industry. Engineers and scientists took the resources, changed them with chemical reactions, and produced materials such as plastic and gasoline.

The presence of oil in Texas had long been suspected. Indians along the coast and near Nacogdoches used asphalt from seepages to waterproof their baskets, and tar balls from offshore seeps washed onto the beaches. This leakage, as well as a sulphur smell that settlers detected in water wells, indicated the presence of petroleum. Near Nacogdoches, Lyne T. Barret, a merchant inspired by oil drilling in Pennsylvania, used a spiral drilling tool in 1866 to find underground oil. He clamped this auger to the end of a pipe and rotated it with a steam engine. He drilled 106 feet deep and touched a small pool, but this shallow well and another found the next year were of little use. That was because there was yet no large market for the petroleum. This situation changed toward the end of the 19th century, however, when chemists learned to convert crude petroleum into kerosene that could be burned in lamps, into lubricants for machinery, and into gasoline that could be used in automobiles.

Other wells produced oil in Brown and Hicks counties. In 1890 Oil Springs, just east of Nacogdoches, claimed 40 wells and a small refinery that processed the petroleum into kerosene. There was further development in Corsicana in 1894, when the town wanted water and hired a man to drill for it. He went down 1,030 feet with his pipe and hit oil. This annoyed him, because he had to continue on down to 2,470 feet to find the water. Corsicana,

After fire destroyed the old capitol in 1881, a new one built of Texas red granite was completed in 1888. Here, workers pose in front of the completed building with the statue The Goddess of Liberty, *which was placed atop the capitol dome.*

however, developed a small oil field that by 1900 had 350 wells producing 836,000 barrels of oil per year.

The early prospectors, known as wildcatters, were people who risked money drilling in places that looked like they might produce oil. It was a guessing game, and they often missed. The first attempt in Texas, in 1865 by Edward von Hartin, was a failure, a "dry hole." Anthony F. Lucas, however, was an expert at guessing. He was born in Austria in 1855 and emigrated to the United States in 1879. He worked for a while as an engineer in a salt mine in Louisiana and learned about salt domes. In 1899 Lucas leased some land at a salt dome near Beaumont where there were surface leakages of petroleum. Two years later Lucas and his workmen drilled the most

Trost

famous oil well in Texas history, Spindletop. Allen W. Hamill, who was one of the workers, commented about the "gusher":

> At about 700 feet or a little over in, why the drilling mud commenced to boil up through the rotary, and it got higher and higher and higher up through the top of the derrick and with such pressure, why the drill pipe commenced to move up. It moved up and started to going out through the top of the derrick. . . . It didn't last so awful long, but it died down very gradually. Well, we three boys then sneaked back down to the well after it quieted down and surveyed the situation. . . . I walked over and looked down the hole there. I heard—sorta heard something kinda bubbling just a little bit and looked down there and here this frothy oil was starting up. But it was just breathing like, you know, coming up and sinking back with the gas pressure. And it kept coming up and over the rotary table and each flow a little higher. Finally it got—came up with such momentum that it just shot up clear through the top of the derrick.

The underground pool had so much pressure in it that when the pipe touched it, gas and oil blew through the hole. In the next six days the well sprayed 500,000 barrels of oil like a black fountain. Finally, workmen capped the well and directed the flow into storage tanks.

This event started a boom as businessmen rushed to make money from the oil bonanza. Petroleum speculators traveled back and forth between Beaumont and Houston. They feverishly traded the papers of oil properties—stocks and oil leases—on the streets and slept on cots in crowded

Oil workers operate the drill used by Anthony F. Lucas at Spindletop.

As "oil fever" infected Texas, boomtowns spread throughout the state. In 1919, oilmen set up a bustling sidewalk stock market in Wichita Falls.

hotel hallways. Beaumont, once a sleepy lumber town of 9,000 people, became a boom town as its population jumped to 50,000 in a few months' time. New companies destined to make petroleum history emerged from the confusion—Gulf Oil Company, Texaco, and Humble Oil and Refining Company.

The gusher made headlines in the newspapers of the nation and changed the Texas economy. From then on, petroleum was the most important product and cotton was second. In 1901 the state approved 491 new oil companies, while the busy drillers made the salt domes look like pincushions. More gushers occurred, and soon the oilmen were finding more than people could use. At one point in this early history a barrel of oil sold for three cents in the oil patch, as a field was sometimes called, while a cup of water sold for five cents.

There were rapid improvements in drilling technology, the manner in which people found oil. In 1850 well diggers simply pounded a steel-tipped pipe into the ground. More useful, it was shortly discovered, was to rotate a pipe with a jagged end. As the serrated end tore up the ground, the drillers flushed out the dirt, or tailings, with water and mud. This led to rotary rigs—or derricks—to turn the pipe, and special end pieces—drill bits—to grind the rock.

One night in a saloon Howard R. Hughes, an oilman, bought a new kind of bit from Granville A. Humason, an oil-field inventor. It had special revolving cones that could eat through rock 10 times faster than other drill bits. Hughes and a partner, Walter B. Sharp, set up a company to manufacture the new piece of equipment. When Hughes died in 1924 his tool company was worth $2 million. This was the foundation of the fortune of his famous son, Howard R. Hughes, Jr., who became one of the richest men in the world.

Other inventions and ideas helped the industry. James Abercrombie of Houston produced a device to prevent blowouts like Spindletop, and geologist Everette Lee DeGolyer of Oklahoma used the science of geophysics to decrease the number of dry holes. Steel derricks and metal storage tanks replaced those made of wood as drillers tapped into deeper pools. Wells descended 4,000 feet deep in 1930, but with stronger pipes, better drill bits, and more powerful rigs wells today sometimes reach a depth of 20,000 feet.

Refineries to process the oil into products like gasoline were set up near the oil discoveries. J. S. Cullinan, an experienced

The vast Goose Creek Oil Field in 1919, with oil derricks stretching across the horizon.

petroleum businessman from Pennsylvania, built a refinery at Corsicana in 1898, and others appeared in Beaumont and Port Arthur. By 1925 there were 80 refineries in Texas. "Oil fever," meanwhile, infected the state as the wildcatters fanned out over the countryside looking for black gold. In the 10 years after Spindletop they found oil at Brownwood, Sour Lake, Wichita Falls, Humble, and on the Waggoner Ranch in North Texas. William T. Waggoner and his father had made a fortune in the cattle business with a ranch that reached 30 miles east and west and 25 miles north and south. Waggoner wanted water for his cattle and was disappointed when the drillers found oil instead.

Discoveries continued: Electra in 1911, Burkburnett in 1912, Goose Creek in 1916, Ranger and Desdemona in 1917, Breckenridge in 1918, Mexia in 1920, Luling in 1922, the Panhandle from 1918 to 1926, the Permian Basin from 1921 to 1929. In 1928 Texas became the leading oil-producing state in the nation, and there was more to come.

In 1930 Columbus Marvin Joiner, a poor but experienced driller from Oklahoma, brought in a successful well in a place where geologists said there was no oil. His East Texas well, 3,580 feet down in deep sand, was in an unusual kind of underground formation. The field he uncovered,

it was later revealed, crossed through five counties and was one of the richest in the world. In just two years drillers completed 5,600 wells around Kilgore and Longview, and Joiner, who was looked upon as the "father" of the East Texas field, was nicknamed "Dad." He needed money, however, and early in the development sold out to H. L. Hunt of Dallas. Hunt went on to become one of the world's richest oilmen, while "Dad" Joiner was almost broke when he died 17 years later.

The oil bonanza produced wealthy land owners and boomtowns. Little farming villages near the oil strikes were quickly overwhelmed when the drillers came to town. In Borger, for example, "Bing" Maddox, a young woman living there at the time, observed: "Borger was like most all boomtowns. It was made up of corrugated sheet iron buildings, tents, one-by-twelve hunter shacks, people living in their automobiles and trailers . . . and some of them even digging holes back under the caprock and living in caves and half-dugouts."

Streets were unpaved, the water supplies and sewage control were uncertain, and the social life was raw. In Borger within eight months 45,000 people arrived to hunt for oil. The town became known for its crime and wild ways, and in 1929 Texas Rangers

had to go to Borger to clear out the criminals. The jail overflowed. The Rangers then handcuffed the prisoners to a chain strung along the main street and invited law officers from around the Southwest to inspect the chained men and claim their crooks.

Frank Hamer, one of the last famous Rangers, helped to tame Borger. He was a fearless man who had been wounded 17 times. Four times he was hurt so badly that doctors thought he would die. Hamer was described by a biographer as "a giant of a man, moon-faced, always in boots, and as talkative as an oyster." In 1934 he caught and killed Bonnie Parker and Clyde Barrow, who had robbed banks and murdered people all across North Texas.

Again, as in the first decade of the 20th century, the oil people were too successful. More petroleum was being produced in the 1930s than could be used, and the price dropped from $1.10 per barrel to 10 cents. This caused a struggle between people who wanted to make as much money as possible in a short time and those who wanted to move more slowly. The conservationists, who wanted to move slowly, knew that a field would produce more oil if allowed to empty over a long period of time. The waste and rapid decline of the fields at Ranger, Desdemona, and Breckenridge had demonstrated the wisdom of conservation.

In the East Texas field, however, at the time the prices for oil were going down the drillers were completing 12 wells per day. After wide discussion in the newspapers and legislature in 1931 Governor Ross S. Sterling ordered the operators of wells to shut down. Sterling sent the National Guard into East Texas to enforce the order. The state then worked out a proration, or schedule of rotation, which meant that the producers took turns letting their wells pump oil. Prices jumped upward as a result and returned decent profits to the industry. This led to illegal pumping, however, and the sale of this so-called hot oil to the refineries. To stop it, Sterling required the refineries to be open for inspection, assigned the Texas Railroad Commission to be certain the proration was observed, and told the Texas Rangers to back up the commission. These actions brought the overproduction under control and marked the beginning of serious efforts to conserve oil in Texas.

Because the Lone Star State was the leading oil producer in the world by the end of the 1930s, the decisions about oil production made by the commission had worldwide impact. If Texas produced more petroleum, the price of gasoline for automobiles would drop. If Texas produced less oil, then the prices would rise. These price changes affected car owners,

Frank Hamer, one of the last famous Texas Rangers, was assigned by Governor Miriam Ferguson to track down the notorious outlaws Bonnie Parker and Clyde Barrow. After three months, he trapped and killed the pair, earning a special citation from the U.S. Congress.

In August 1915, the S.S. Satilla *became the first deep-water ship to carry freight up Houston's new ship channel. By the 1920s, the Port of Houston had surpassed the Port of Galveston in amount of freight carried in and out.*

oil companies, refineries, tax revenues for governments, and oil-well owners.

Texas oil production continued to rise until 1972, then began a slow decline as the oil supply dwindled. Not many new fields were uncovered after the 1930s. The business nevertheless had a far-reaching impact on Texas life. People moved to the Lone Star State to work in the industry, and the money produced by oil raised wages and the prices of land.

Houston blossomed like a magnolia tree in the early 1900s. The city was in the right place at the right time for the oil bonanza. Houston leaders had dreamed of a ship channel to make the inland city a seaport. The United States government supported the idea and sent the Army Corps of Engineers to dredge Buffalo Bayou, the stream that led to Houston. The engineers also dug a channel through Galveston Bay and placed a large basin at Harrisburg on Buffalo Bayou, near Houston, so that ships could turn around. After the engineers completed a channel 25 feet deep in 1914, President

Woodrow Wilson fired a cannon by remote control from Washington, D.C., for the opening ceremony. The daughter of the Houston mayor sprinkled white rose petals into the turning basin, announcing, "I christen thee Port Houston, hither the boats of all nations may come and receive hearty welcome."

Further improvements took place after this time. The Houston Ship Channel eventually was expanded to more than 40 feet deep and 300 feet wide. Houston thus became a deep-water port where the largest transport ships could dock. By the 1920s, the Port of Houston surpassed its rival, the Port of Galveston, in tons of products moved. Oil shipments eventually placed Houston among the top four ports in the nation.

The long ship channel attracted companies that wanted a harbor safe from hurricanes, and by 1930 fifty companies, including a fertilizer division of Armour and Company, Texas Portland Cement, American Maid Flour, and the Texas Chemical Company, had located there. Pipelines brought oil to the area, and by 1930 there were eight refineries on its banks. Oil companies established regional headquarters in Houston and people poured into the city, pushing its population ahead of Dallas and San Antonio. Houston has remained the largest city in Texas ever since.

Even though the city had no nearby oil fields, Dallas became important in North Texas. Using its network of railroads, Dallas business people found success in banking, cotton dealing, insurance, and

clothing manufacturing. One of the more interesting clothing companies was started in 1938 by Elsie Frankfurt, who noticed that her older sister had no stylish clothes to wear after she became pregnant. Expectant women wore wraparound garments or dresses several sizes too large. Frankfurt, who could sew well, designed and made a special skirt and jacket for her sister. The clothes brought so many compliments that Frankfurt and her sisters went into business producing attractive Page Boy clothes for pregnant women. When movie stars began to wear the clothing, Elsie Frankfurt became a nationwide success.

Another Dallas success story involved Joseph M. Haggar, an immigrant from Lebanon. He set up factories in small Texas towns to make "slacks," pants that men could wear in their slack, or nonworking time. During World War II, Haggar made uniforms for the military; after the war he expanded the business to produce a variety of men's clothing for national distribution. In Fort Worth in the prewar years, Charles N. Williamson and Emmett E. Dickie made heavy-duty work clothes called "Dickies." They also made uniforms in World War II.

The largest clothing maker, however, was Mansour "Frank" Farah, like Haggar a Lebanese immigrant. In 1920 Farah started a family business in El Paso to make work shirts and denim pants. Over the next half century his successful company expanded statewide and grew to employ 12,000 people. Like Haggar, the Farah label is now distributed through department stores nationwide.

Textile workers operate laundry dryers in a Dallas factory around 1910. Dallas developed into a center specializing in ready-made clothing. In Dallas and elsewhere, textile labor consisted mainly of women earning low wages.

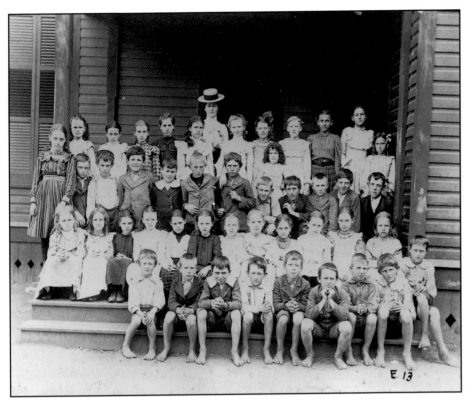

Barefoot but eager, the schoolchildren of the Cleburne public school pose with their teacher. In the early part of the 20th century, state officials tried to enhance the quality of rural schools by consolidating them. By 1930, some 1,500 schools had merged.

Annie Webb Blanton, an Austin schoolteacher, was elected superintendent of public instruction in 1918. She supported woman suffrage and worked to expand the opportunities available to women educators.

For the most part, however, Texas manufacturing efforts lagged behind the rest of the United States until World War II; the economic strength of Texas was in the production of oil, cotton, and cattle. These were extractive, rural enterprises and, as might be expected, the majority of Texans still lived in the countryside. In 1920 about half the people in the United States lived in cities; Texas did not reach that point until the 1940s.

In still other areas of life, changes tended to lag behind the rest of the nation. With the economy booming, however, Texans began to pay more attention to social reform. For example, Thomas M. Campbell, who was governor from 1907 to 1911, altered prison policies and supported higher standards in schools. Prisoners were often whipped, rented out to businessmen as laborers, and forced to wear uniforms with large black and white stripes. Campbell ended those practices. The public schools in Texas cities were much like those elsewhere in the nation—the white ones, at least—but the rural schools were far worse. None of the country schools had enough money or teachers. Campbell and others supported the movement to merge the

rural schools to make them better, and by 1930 1,500 schools had consolidated. This movement allowed a concentration of resources, and it continued as more of the population moved to the cities.

In 1915 the legislature ordered school attendance for all children from 8 to 14 years of age, and it required them to stay in school for at least 60 days per year. The legislature soon changed these rules, making attendance mandatory from ages 6 to 16 for 180 days. In 1918 Texas began to provide free books to students. Annie Webb Blanton, an Austin schoolteacher who worked for both better education and women's right to vote, was elected superintendent of public instruction in 1918. The first woman in Texas to win a state office, she later commented, "While I had the friendly help of many good men, there was always a faction of narrow prejudices who opposed everything that I attempted, not because there was no merit in what I was seeking, but because of the fact that the one initiating it was a woman." Margie Neal, the first woman senator in Texas, introduced the bill that created the State Board of Education in 1929. Thereafter, because of the work of Blanton and Neal, Texas had a stronger school system.

Governor Campbell was followed in office by Oscar B. Colquitt, who continued the reforms from 1911 to 1915. Colquitt backed improvement in the state hospitals and sought laws to make factories safer for children and women.

Colquitt was followed by James E. Ferguson, one of the most colorful chief executives in Texas history. "Farmer Jim," as he was called, was the son of a poor Methodist minister in Bell County. Ferguson became a lawyer, farmer, and banker before he decided to run, with no political experience, for the governor's position. He nonetheless spoke up in favor of helping tenant farmers—people who worked on rented farmland—and against Prohibition. There was in Texas and elsewhere in the nation a long-standing movement against drunkenness. Advocates of Prohibition wanted to prohibit, or ban, the sale of all alcoholic drinks, such as whiskey, gin, wine, and beer. Those people who favored Prohibition were called "drys," while those who were against it were called "wets." Ferguson was a "wet" who talked to his audiences with earthy, crude language.

In his first two years in office (1915–17) Governor Ferguson tried without success to aid the tenant farmers, failed to halt the coming of Prohibition, took a stand against the Ku Klux Klan—an organization that promoted Anglo social supremacy—and started the State Department of Forestry. Along with concerns about wasted oil, this regard for the forests marks the beginning of conservation in Texas, part of a national movement reaching back to the Forest Reserve Act of 1891 and the days of Theodore Roosevelt's Presidency (1901–9). The basic idea of conservation was to preserve, restore, and use wisely the limited natural resources of the country. Ferguson did not really understand the issue. It was actually the work of W. Goodrich Jones, a businessman and banker, who convinced the governor of the wisdom of the idea.

While touring Germany, Jones observed the value of reforestation, or planting new trees after a forest has been cut. At his home in Temple, Texas, he planted hackberry trees along the streets to give shade to the residents. For his efforts, this small, bespectacled man was called a "tree crank" and had to endure the nickname "Hackberry Jones." Jones nonetheless started a forestry club to promote interest in trees and asked the state for money. He wanted a department of forestry to look after the trees of the state. Ferguson misunderstood. "Why do you need $10,000? Why, for $500 I can get you a good man to cut all the trees you want," said the governor. Jones did not want to cut trees—he wanted to grow them. "Hackberry Jones" finally got what

Governor Jim Ferguson and his wife, Miriam, meet the public. Ferguson's folksy, earthy language appealed to voters, who elected him governor in 1915. After his banishment from public office, "Pa" Ferguson offered his wife to the voters. "Two governors for the price of one," he said. He thus lived up to his motto, "Never say 'die,' say 'damn!'"

Pancho Villa (far left), one of the leaders of the Mexican Revolution, relaxes with one of his generals in an El Paso restaurant in 1911. Villa had established his headquarters in an El Paso office building.

he wanted for the good of the state, the State Department of Forestry, through the legislature.

The Texas Highway Department also began in a quiet way during Ferguson's tenure. In 1916 the U.S. Congress offered funding for the building of roads if the states would provide an equal amount. To take advantage of this legislation, Texas had to create the new department in 1917. Before this time the construction and maintenance of roads had been left to the counties, resulting in uneven quality. This was a chance to have a standard system in which the roads would all be the same. Unfortunately, there were management problems in the highway department and not enough money to do much. In 1930 there were only 7,300 miles of paved roads in Texas— barely enough to connect the larger towns. In 1940 there were 19,000 miles, including an increasing number of farm-to-town

roads, and in 1950 there were 54,000 miles, which covered the state with two-lane highways.

Ferguson got into trouble because he tried to fire professors at the University of Texas who had spoken against him during his second election campaign in 1916. When the board of regents, which controlled the university, refused to banish the teachers, Ferguson blocked the funding of the school. At the same time, Ferguson's opponents brought charges that he had illegally borrowed money and misused public funds. The Senate held an impeachment trial on these charges that lasted three weeks, and the members voted 25 to 3 to remove Ferguson as governor. The impeachment, the first and only such trial of a governor in Texas history, also banned him from ever holding a state office again.

While these political fireworks were going off in Austin, there were real fireworks going off elsewhere. Mexico plunged into a series of revolts over control of the country. Hoping to embroil the United States in a war with Mexico, Pancho Villa, one of the rebels, led raids across the border of the United States. In 1916 Villa murdered some Americans he had kidnapped from a Mexican train and then killed 19 more in a raid on Columbus, New Mexico. Consequently, with the permission of the Mexican government President Woodrow Wilson sent an expedition from San Antonio into Mexico to capture Villa. The army, led by General John J. "Blackjack" Pershing, came home empty-handed, the outlaw continued to raid into Texas, and Wilson ordered troops to guard the border.

Detachment of U.S. Cavalry ... Villa

This was a part of a low-level conflict along the border that flared from 1915 to 1918. The irritation came from old, simmering hatreds between Texans and Mexicans, the movement of Anglo-American farmers into the Rio Grande Valley, the brutality of the Texas Rangers, and attacks on Texans by Mexican bandits. The history is unclear and full of shadows. It is thought, however, that citizens without authority (vigilantes) and law officers killed as many as 3,000 Mexicans in the valley during this period. U.S. troops were assigned to Brownsville after 1914 to keep the peace.

Beginning in 1914, there was also conflict in Europe. The Allies (Great Britain, France, Italy, and Russia) lined up to fight the Central Powers (Germany, Austria-Hungary, and Turkey) in World War I. The United States remained neutral until 1917. Then, led by President Wilson, the country entered the war on the side of the

Allies "to make the world safe for democracy." Texas became a training ground for American troops at Camp MacArthur in Waco, Camp Logan in Houston, Camp Bowie in Fort Worth, and Camp Travis in San Antonio.

About 200,000 Texans joined the armed services, and about 5,000 of them died during the war. Other patriotic Texans saved food, bought war bonds, and learned to hate everything connected with Germany, the chief enemy. Governor Will Hobby, who led the state from 1917 to 1921, went so far as to cancel the funding for German-language study at the University of Texas. The study of German was also stopped in the high schools. This sort of action took place all over the country, and Americans even changed the name of sauerkraut to "liberty cabbage." This was particularly sad in a state like Texas, which had a heritage of German immigration. As

The United States sent troops—including this Seventh Cavalry detachment—into Mexico to hunt down Pancho Villa. But the troops returned home empty-handed and Villa's raids continued.

At Camp Dick, an English sergeant major instructs a World War I recruit on the proper way to use a bayonet.

World War I provided a boost to the Texas economy. Here, workers at Steves Sash and Door Company in San Antonio make airplane propellers.

Officers of the "Buffalos," 367th Infantry, 77th Division, in France around 1918.

a consequence of the war, study about Texas-German culture was largely ignored for five decades. In 1968, however, the films and exhibits presented at the San Antonio HemisFair about Texas cultures inspired renewed interest in the German legacy of art, architecture, music, cooking, and language.

The war brought useful outside money and people to Texas for combat preparation, but it stirred the ethnic pot in ugly ways. The demons of prejudice were never far away, with or without warfare. Northern black soldiers, unused to the segregation they found in Texas, clashed with citizens in Brownsville, San Antonio, and Del Rio, and worst of all in Houston. African-American soldiers had been assigned guard duty while workers built Camp Logan on the

west side of town. The soldiers hated the segregation in Houston, the lack of respect from Houston police, and being called "nigger" by white people in town.

The arrest of a soldier for drunkenness and the rumor that he had been killed set off a riot. Seventy-five black troopers grabbed their guns and shot up the town. Law authorities struck back with Coast Guard soldiers from Galveston and troops from San Antonio. As a result, 19 people died and 11 more were wounded. The black soldiers were brought to trial in military courts and 19 of them died by execution. The other soldiers involved were sent to prison and later dishonorably discharged from the army.

The war also launched Texas and the nation into Prohibition. Temperance, or refraining from drinking alcohol, had been

The women of Lufkin (left) gather in 1915 to urge the passage of Prohibition statutes. As soon as Prohibition became law in 1918, smugglers and bootleggers set out to sidestep it. At top, a Mexican smuggles alcohol across the Rio Grande. Below, customs officers empty confiscated liquor into the river.

an issue in Texas since the days of Sam Houston. Baptist and Methodist churches were especially active against people getting drunk, and a Texas law in effect since 1866 closed all saloons on Sundays. Even the most famous woman temperance worker, Carrie Nation, visited the state. Smashing windows, mirrors, and bottles with bricks, she demolished a bar in Houston that had been sarcastically named in her honor. In Galveston she went into a saloon and said to the drinkers, "There you go pouring out some of that slop. Men, you ought not to drink that stuff, it will ruin your liver and damn your souls."

Still, prohibition groups were a minority until World War I. Attitudes changed then because Americans thought it necessary to protect young soldiers from alcohol. In 1917 Texas passed a law banning saloons within 10 miles of military camps. Shortly thereafter the Texas legislature endorsed the 18th Amendment to the U.S. Constitution, which made it illegal to manufacture, sell, or transport intoxicating liquor. In spite of the good intentions and the efforts of police, the Prohibition law could not be enforced. Americans contin-

ued to enjoy alcoholic drinks that they made at home or bought from bootleggers or smugglers.

The Texas coast, particularly Galveston Island, became a place for smuggling the illegal liquor. Ships from England filled with bottles of whiskey and gin anchored just outside the legal limits of the United States, where they were met by bootleggers in small, fast speedboats. The bootleggers brought the bottles to the island, transferred them to trains and trucks, and sold them to customers as far inland as Cleveland and Detroit.

Smugglers amassed fortunes, and rival gangs fought for control. From this situation emerged Sam and Rosario Maceo, who took over illegal gambling and liquor sales in Galveston from the 1920s to the 1950s. Although it was against the law, the brothers opened nightclubs and offered both gambling and liquor. They were able to continue so long as the people of Texas thought their business was not as bad as the laws. The Texas authorities left Galveston alone for 30 years.

World War I brought not only Prohibition but also women's right to vote. Early

To show support for woman suffrage in Texas, three men pull a woman on a tractor. In 1918, the Texas Constitution was amended to allow women to vote in primary elections. The next year, the 19th Amendment to the U.S. Constitution was ratified, granting women the right to vote in national elections.

MIRIAM A. FERGUSON
Candidate for Governor
SECOND TERM
SUBJECT TO THE ACTION OF THE DEMOCRATIC PRIMARY, JULY 24, 1926

1. Read what Ferguson-ism has done for Texas.

2. A man who will not read both sides of a question is dishonest.—Abraham Lincoln.

3. Do not send a boy to mill.

4. The State is now on a cash basis, and there is money in the Treasury.

5. The penitentiary is paying its way.

6. Taxes have been reduced.

7. No strikes or lynchings.

8. The schools are being run economically and efficiently.

9. The insane have been taken out of jails.

10. Mercy and forgiveness is extended to the friendless and unfortunate.

11. All these a woman Governor has brought to Texas.

12. Why change?

Governor Miriam A. "Ma" Ferguson, the wife of former governor Jim Ferguson, served two terms as governor of Texas. She was the first woman ever elected governor in the United States.

Governor Will Hobby, the lieutenant governor who had taken office after the impeachment of James Ferguson, took up the cause and obtained legislative approval for women to vote in primary elections. In return, women's groups worked for his election in 1918 and he won easily. In 1919, during its regular session, the legislature approved the 19th Amendment to the United States Constitution. This amendment gave women the right to vote in national elections; Texas led all other southern states on this issue. In 1924 Miriam "Ma" Ferguson, the wife of banned ex-governor Jim Ferguson, became the first elected woman governor in the nation. She was elected again in 1932 during the worst part of the Great Depression.

The entire nation suffered during the depression. Banks and other businesses closed, and about one-fourth of the working people lost their jobs. There were no new jobs, people could not pay their bills, and some families ran out of food. Three children starved to death in Lubbock, and the town leaders plowed the grass lawn of city hall into a turnip garden to feed people. Fort Worth and Wichita Falls had to sell the animals in their zoos. Churches and civic organizations tried to feed people, but these groups also ran out of money.

In West Texas the situation was made worse by grasshoppers and drought. It was so dry that nothing would grow, and great clouds of dust swept over the countryside. The air was so dirty that at times it blocked out the sun, and in May 1934 dust from West Texas, Oklahoma, Colorado, and Kansas blew all the way eastward to settle

women's groups had petitioned the 1868 and 1875 Texas constitutional conventions for the franchise, the right to vote. These efforts failed, but the cause was again taken up by the Texas Woman Suffrage Association, started in Galveston and Houston in 1903. Led by Minnie Fisher Cunningham of Galveston and Annie Webb Blanton of Austin, this association and others petitioned for voting privileges in 1915 and 1917.

A cigar box from the 1932 Vice Presidential campaign of John Nance "Cactus Jack" Garner.

President Franklin D. Roosevelt congratulates Lyndon B. Johnson (right) after his election to Congress in 1937.

on the desks of politicians in Washington, D.C. In 1932 writer John Fischer drove his car from Oklahoma City to Amarillo while a norther with a 50-mile-per-hour wind roared over the plains. Fischer wore a wet bandanna over his mouth and nose so that he could breathe. When he reached Amarillo he discovered that the right side of his car had been blasted by the sand right down to bright metal. There was no paint left.

In the national elections of 1932 the country voted for Franklin D. Roosevelt and the Democrats. Americans wanted action against the depression, and Roosevelt was willing to try. His answer was the New Deal, a large number of new laws and programs designed to create jobs and to revive the economy. Texas had powerful friends in Washington, D.C., specifically Vice President John Nance "Cactus Jack" Garner, who was from Uvalde, and Jesse H. Jones. Jones, a Houston businessman who served as the director of the Reconstruction Finance Corporation, disbursed enormous amounts of money for the revival of business, particularly banks. At one time he was overheard to say about a project, "I'll not give a nickel more than two billion dollars for it!" Garner and Jones made certain that Texas got its share of federal government aid.

Welcomed by Governor Ferguson and other Texas politicians, the New Deal spent about $1.5 billion in Texas. The money was used to build roads, bridges, public buildings, and parks. The San Jacinto Monument at the battleground near Houston, the tower of the Main Building at the University of Texas at Austin, the River Walk in downtown San Antonio, Lamar High School in Houston, and the dams on the Colorado River were all New Deal projects. The Federal Writers' Project hired jobless scholars to write city histories and to organize archives, special libraries for letters and government records. Poor artists were hired to paint murals in public buildings, and in so doing they helped develop a special style of southwestern art.

Lyndon B. Johnson, destined to become President of the United States, got his start during the Great Depression first as an assistant to Congressman Richard Kleberg of Corpus Christi in 1932 and then as state administrator of the National Youth Administration in 1935. After Congressman James Buchanan died in 1937, Johnson won election to the seat over eight rivals by becoming a champion of the New Deal in Texas. President Franklin D. Roosevelt, touring the state at the time, took notice of Johnson's effort. He rewarded him by obtaining Johnson's appointment to the House Committee on Naval Affairs, a major step up for a new congressman.

The Great Depression ended with World War II. In 1939, under the leadership of Adolf Hitler, Germany invaded Poland. France and Great Britain tried to help Poland, but the Germans quickly defeated France and turned on the Soviet Union. The Soviets and the British then became allies against the Germans and the Italians, who had joined together to become the Axis Powers. On December 7, 1941, the Japanese surprised the United States with an attack on the naval fleet at Pearl Harbor in Hawaii. During the attack Dorie Miller, a

A ferocious dust storm swept through Perryton on April 14, 1935.

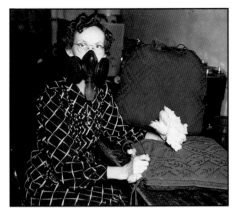

The New Deal came to Texas during the Great Depression. At left, a woman employee of the Works Progress Administration restores furniture in San Antonio's City Hall. Below, the Civilian Conservation Corps constructs a lookout tower in Big Bend Park.

military; 23,000 were killed in action. They served on land and sea in all the theaters of the war and 30 won the Congressional Medal of Honor for bravery.

At home, people participated in war-bond drives, air-raid drills, rationing, memorial services for those who died, and the production of war supplies. Texans restricted their use of vital war materials, such as gasoline and tires, through ration-ing, and dug up their flower beds to plant vegetables in "victory gardens." During air-raid drills, people turned off their lights at night or put tight black shades on their windows. These "blackouts" made it hard for a city to be seen from the air. At schools children were taught to go into hallways, basements, or under desks during the drills. When the war finally ended—the Germans surrendered on May 7, 1945, and the Japa-nese surrendered on August 14, 1945—there were celebrations throughout Texas, as there were throughout the nation. Audie Murphy, of Farmersville, Texas, was perhaps the most celebrated war hero in America. In an autobiography published in 1949, he wrote:

> When I was a child, I was told that men were branded by war. Has the brand been put on me? Have the years of blood and ruin stripped me of all decency? Of all belief?
>
> Not all belief. I believe in the force of a hand grenade, the power of artillery, the accuracy of a Garand [rifle]. I believe in hitting before you get hit, and that dead men do not look noble.... We have been so in-tent on death that we have forgotten life. And now suddenly life faces us. I swear to myself that I will measure

black Texas seaman, grabbed a machine gun and shot down four Japanese airplanes. He won the Navy Cross for his action. The United States thus joined with the Soviet Union and Great Britain in the fight against Germany, Italy, and Japan.

There was so much to be done to fight the war that everyone found jobs to do. Some men and women joined the armed services, while others went to work at home to produce food, uniforms, ships, and air-planes. The good weather in Texas was favorable for the location of training camps, and the federal government built 15 army bases and 40 airfields. About 750,000 Texas men and 12,000 women joined the

The good citizens of Elgin organized a scrap metal drive in 1942.

Audie Murphy: To Hell and Back

In just 28 months during World War II an unusual Texan, Audie Murphy, won every U.S. Army medal for bravery. He came from a small northeast Texas farm and weighed only 110 pounds when he entered the army. He relished the discipline of military life and quickly rose through the ranks from private to lieutenant.

Murphy won the Congressional Medal of Honor for stopping a German attack of six tanks and infantry in 1945. He had ordered his men to take cover in a wood, and then went by himself with a radio to an advanced position to tell artillerymen where to fire. While there the Germans came up to his position and Murphy climbed on top of a burning American tank destroyer. He rolled the dead commander out into the snow and began to fire its heavy machine guns. Murphy killed or wounded 50 German soldiers and did not retreat to the woods with the other American soldiers until he ran out of bullets. The burning tank destroyer then exploded. The Texan refused treatment for an old wound that had reopened and rallied his men to a counterattack until the Germans retreated.

After winning more medals than any other soldier in the war, Audie Murphy returned home a hero in June 1945, greeted by parades in Dallas, San Antonio, and his hometown of Farmersville. At this time he was not quite 21 years old. Afterward he wrote a book about his war adventures entitled To Hell and Back *and made several Hollywood movies. He died in an airplane crash in 1971.*

up to it. I may be branded by war, but I will not be defeated by it.... I will learn to look at life through uncynical eyes, to have faith, to know love. I will learn to work in peace as in war. And finally—finally, like countless others, I will learn to live again.

The war brought great growth and change to Texas. Houston was at the center of a region of natural resources that were useful for war materials, and factories were set up to make rubber from petroleum. The rubber was then turned into tires, lifeboats, and dirigibles in Akron, Ohio. Natural gas from wells became useful for heating purposes and large pipelines were built from Texas to the East Coast. At Houston, Beaumont, and Orange shipyards built ships for

the U.S. Navy and employed thousands of workers. At the same time, Dallas and Fort Worth built airplanes, and San Antonio trained the pilots.

During the 1940s Texas grew by 20 percent, with every fifth person a newcomer. For the first time, the number of people living in the countryside declined as the cities doubled in size. By 1950 three-fifths of the Texas population lived in urban regions. Texans themselves grew in experience and worldliness. Soldiers had gone to war, traveled to faraway places, seen other ways of living, and returned to joyous celebrations when World War II ended in 1945. The soldiers and the newcomers had seen a larger world, and Texas became a different place.

The skyline of Dallas looms up from flat grasslands. Built with profits from cotton and petroleum, the city's skyscrapers identify Dallas as a major commercial center.

Chapter Six

Texas and the World

On St. Patrick's Day 1949 Glenn McCarthy, a wildcat oil millionaire, opened his new Shamrock Hotel in Houston. It was 18 stories high and decorated in 63 shades of green. He invited 175 movie stars and 50,000 people to the event. Dorothy Lamour, a Hollywood movie actress, was scheduled to broadcast her radio show from the hotel ballroom. The crowds became so dense at the opening reception that it took 30 minutes just to cross the lobby. Some people got stuck in the entrance and the mayor of Houston had to wait two hours to get inside.

The noise in the ballroom was so great that the actors had to shout to be heard. Unknown voices cut into the broadcast, while people in the crowded ballroom grabbed the microphone and hooted into it. The National Broadcasting Company finally cut the show off the air. This scene of outrageous behavior became a model for an incident in Edna Ferber's best-selling book about Texas, *Giant*. The book and the movie based on it supported a myth believed by many outsiders that Texans were rich, crude, loud, and aggressive.

Giant also portrayed Texas as a state dominated by white, racially prejudiced men. The television show "Dallas," which ran from 1978 to 1991, reflected the same attitudes and was broadcast around the world. These were modern variants of the "wild west" image long in use in movies, stories, and books. This Texas image, however, was misleading and did not come close to giving a complete description of modern Texas, a land that was transformed after World War II by returning soldiers, newcomers, and a surging economy based on oil production.

Nonetheless, much of the myth began at home. Three writers at the University of Texas supported, explored, and helped to define it—J. Frank Dobie, a folklorist; Walter Prescott Webb, a historian; and Roy Bedichek, a naturalist. They lived and worked together in Austin for 30 years after World War I. Close friends, they met once a month at Dobie's ranch in the nearby hill country and sat around a campfire. There they told stories into the late hours and tested each other with ideas.

Webb wrote about the Texas frontier and the Texas Rangers. He said, "The real

Historian Walter Prescott Webb and folklorist J. Frank Dobie supported and nurtured the Texas mystique.

Willie Nelson's music helped to bring country-western music to the attention of the rest of the country.

Ranger has been a very quiet, deliberate, gentle person who could gaze calmly into the eye of a murderer, divine his thoughts, and anticipate his action, a man who could ride straight up to death." Bedichek studied the Karankawa Indians and wrote about animals and nature in the Lone Star State. Dobie wrote about lost gold mines, buried treasure, longhorns, and cowboys. "Great literature," said Dobie, "transcends its native land, but none that I know of ignores its own soil." These men all died by the mid-1960s, but their legacy was to capture readers' interest in Texas frontier themes and events. By the end of their careers, Texans had quit being southerners and begun to think of themselves as westerners.

Popular country-western music reflected the change. This music was a combination of cowboy and cotton-farmer songs that reached back to the 1920s. Bob Wills was the most important of the early musicians and his band, the Texas Playboys, continued to entertain people into the 1950s. A later group of Texas artists built on this western music tradition, starting in the 1970s. They were led by Willie Nelson, Jerry Jeff Walker, Michael Murphy, Kris Kristofferson, and Waylon Jennings. Combining western music with rock, blues, and gospel, they performed at places like the Armadillo World Headquarters in Austin and put the Texas myth into music. Willie Nelson's 1975 album *The Red-Headed Stranger* was a good example. It told of love, heartbreak, murder, and lawlessness in a western setting.

At the same time this western theme in music was evolving, however, there were some different notes that reflected the complexity of Texas society. Buddy Holly, a thin man with curly black hair and heavy black-rimmed glasses, began his singing career in Lubbock in 1955. He combined western and early rock rhythms into a rollicking, playful style. In 1957 and 1958 Holly and the Crickets had seven national hits, including "Peggy Sue." Holly's career ended suddenly, however, with his death at age 22 in a 1959 airplane crash. It was a day the "music died," as a later song, "American Pie," stated in tribute to Holly's contribution to rock and roll.

Janis Joplin's singing career also ended abruptly. She was from Port Arthur and ran away from home at age 17 to perform in the honky-tonk western bars of Austin. Although she could not read music, her earthy, plaintive voice brought her fame as a folk singer in the 1960s during the national disturbances over civil rights and the Vietnam War. Her most famous song was "Me and Bobbie McGee," with the unforgettable line "Freedom's just another word for nothin' left to lose." Joplin was rebellious and lonely; she died of a drug overdose in 1970.

Texas cities, meanwhile, with the support of philanthropic business people, made progress in classical music, founding orchestras and opera companies. The Houston Symphony Orchestra, one of the earliest, started in 1913 and steadily improved, particularly under the lead of Ernst Hoffmann from 1936 to 1947. It was not easy for this conductor. He had to deal with a tympanist who smoked a cigar during rehearsals and a bassoonist who played with his shoes off. The orchestra continued to improve under other conductors, including Sir John Barbirolli who led the orchestra on a highly acclaimed tour in 1964.

Dallas, Amarillo, San Antonio, Austin, Midland-Odessa, and Corpus Christi all supported symphony orchestras. Houston, San Antonio, Dallas, and Fort Worth began opera associations. San Antonio was the first to have a professional opera director in 1945. Houston's Grand Opera Association started in 1956 and has since become nationally famous for staging premiere productions of modern works such as *Nixon in China* by John Adams and *Akhnaten* by Philip Glass.

Theater groups also flowered in Texas at mid-century. In Houston, Nina Vance began the Alley Theatre in 1947, with local, small-donor support. This was a repertory theater, a type of theater in which the same resident actors present a series of plays. In Dallas another remarkable woman, Margo Jones, developed the concept of theater-in-the-round, in which the audience was seated in a circle around a circular stage. Her premiere production in 1955 of *Inherit the Wind*, by Jerome Lawrence and Robert E. Lee, traveled from Dallas to Broadway in New York City and marked her success. These accomplishments in literature and the arts, both at the popular and classical levels, indicated a society that was evolving from a struggling, frontier past into a major contributor to national culture.

Recklessness with firearms and the continued use of guns in Texas, however, seemed to indicate that Texans still possessed a problem with its frontier past. In

Vanya! Vanyushka!

In 1957 one of Rosina Lhevinne's students at the Juilliard School of Music in New York handed her a brochure announcing the first Tchaikovsky International Piano and Violin Festival, to be held in Moscow the following year. After reading the brochure she stood, holding it, and studied the fall day through a window. To herself she said softly, "Van."

With that decision she began a successful campaign to find the money to send her brilliant former student Van Cliburn to the competition. He possessed a particular affinity for Russian music, which he played with sweeping majesty, warmth, and technical genius. Cliburn had been born in Shreveport, Louisiana, in 1934 and at age six moved with his parents to Kilgore, Texas, where his father worked as a land agent for the Magnolia Petroleum Company. With his mother as piano teacher, Van showed an early talent. He gave his first public presentation at age four. When he registered for the first grade, his teacher asked if he could read. He replied, "Well, no, ma'am. I can't read writing, but I can read music."

His mother continued to give him music lessons and at an early age Van Cliburn decided to become a concert pianist. His parents provided him with a practice room off the garage with two pianos to go along with the two pianos in the house. Cliburn finished high school in Kilgore, grew to 6 feet, 4 inches tall with a mop of unruly hair to top it off, and went to the Juilliard School of Music. He graduated in 1954 and began to win the leading piano competitions in the United States. One of these was the prestigious Leventritt International Competition, which he won in 1954 and which provided him with concert engagements in New York, Cleveland, Pittsburgh, Buffalo, and Denver.

In spite of this success, Cliburn was practically unknown to the American public until his triumph in Moscow in 1958. There, after playing a repertoire of compositions by Bach, Chopin, Liszt, Rachmaninoff, and of course Tchaikovsky, he won the Tchaikovsky Gold Medal. He was wildly greeted by Russian fans shouting his name, "Vanya! Vanyushka!" and he was formally congratulated by the Soviet premier, Nikita Khrushchev. "Why are you so tall?" asked the short, pudgy Soviet leader. "Because I am from Texas," answered Cliburn.

On his return, the 24-year-old pianist was greeted with a New York City ticker-tape parade in the company of Mayor Robert F. Wagner. At that time America needed a hero. The Soviets had successfully launched the first space satellite, *Sputnik,* in 1957, a feat yet unmatched by the United States. Van Cliburn gave his fellow citizens a victory in the cold war struggle with the Soviets, and he became a national celebrity. He was like a mythical Texas Ranger galloping out of nowhere to banish the enemy and save the day. The attention he received, along with his cordial manners, likable personality, and superb artistry, ensured his later reputation as one of America's most famous pianists. In 1978 he retired to live a reclusive life with scant public interaction except at the Van Cliburn International Piano Competition that started in 1962 in Fort Worth. It was named in his honor by the sponsoring foundation. In 1987 he began to play a few scattered concerts starting with a state dinner at the White House for Soviet premier Mikhail Gorbachev. In 1994, however, he emerged fully from retirement with a 15-city tour and a free performance in Chicago that attracted 350,000 listeners.

Cliburn performs at the Tchaikovsky Festival, 1958.

A rider is thrown from his bull at the Travis County Rodeo. Eight seconds on the bull is considered a successful ride.

By reputation, the most risky of all sports is trying to ride a wild bull. The 1,600-pound animal will try not only to throw the cowboy or cowgirl off its back but also to trample and gore the rider on the ground. Bull games have ancient origins that reach back as far as Minoan civilization, which flourished from about 3000 B.C. to 1100 B.C. on the island of Crete. But modern bull riding is a part of the rodeo.

People who worked with cattle, cowboys and *vaqueros* (*vaquero* is the Spanish word for "cowboy") developed the necessary equestrian skills of roping, branding, herding, and riding.

Competition to test these skills developed in Mexico and moved northward with the development of the cattle industry in the western United States. The contests led first to ranch-versus-ranch rodeos and then to rodeos at county fairs and Fourth of July celebrations in the 1860s. Buffalo Bill Cody, a former bison hunter for the railroads, organized the first professional rodeo in North Platte, Nebraska, in 1882, and began touring the country with his Wild West show the next year. Cody's show, as well as those of numerous imitators, popularized rodeo as a cowboy sport, and

western towns such as Cheyenne, Wyoming; Calgary, Canada; Houston, and Fort Worth organized annual rodeos to celebrate their frontier heritage.

One of the more unusual events was the Texas Prison Rodeo, which started in 1931 at Huntsville. Prisoners with good jail records could participate and attend, and because the prisoners often had little to lose, they rode and roped with careless abandon. The rodeo, which was open to the public, was labeled "Texas's Fastest and Wildest Rodeo." The profits were used for prison educational and recreational programs.

Rodeos mainly featured cowboys in the tough events of bronco riding, steer roping, and bull riding; women participated in less dangerous events, such as barrel racing and trick riding. In 1947, however, Amarillo hosted the first all-girl rodeo. Fern Sawyer of Fort Worth competed in most of the events and was quoted in *Cowgirls: Women of the American West,* by Teresa Jordan:

"I wasn't entered in the bull riding but one night they didn't have anybody to ride a bull cause everybody was hurt. I told them I would do it because the crowd deserved to see a bull ride.... Well, Daddy just had a fit, but I went

down there and got on that bull.... I did ride him, but I broke my hand in nine places. I didn't get bucked off. I broke it gripping so hard. I didn't say anything about my hand, just went and drove my horses home. Pretty soon my hand got about as big as my leg...they had to fly me to Lubbock and put all those bones in place. I'd got seven dollars mount money to ride that bull. That wasn't prize money because I wasn't entered. That's just what they paid me to ride him. Daddy didn't think I'd made very much with that ride because he had to spend about a thousand on my hand."

Buddy Holly (second from right), from Lubbock, had a string of hits in the late 1950s before his death in a plane crash in 1959. He is shown here with his band, the Crickets.

1928, Amon Carter, one of the political leaders of Fort Worth, attended the National Democratic Party Convention in Houston. The packed elevator at the Rice Hotel passed his floor four times. Impatient, Carter grabbed a sheriff's pistol and angrily shot the glass doors of the elevator six times. No one was hurt, and the next time the elevator stopped for him. This was not the sort of behavior that impressed the delegates from the rest of the United States.

One of the worst multiple shootings in modern history, moreover, occurred in 1966 in Austin. Charles Whitman, who had been a marine sharpshooter, apparently went insane. He killed his wife and mother and then, heavily armed, went to the observation deck of the main tower at the University of Texas. There he killed two more people and began shooting at students on the plaza below. He killed 17 people and wounded 30 before two brave policemen and a volunteer stopped him. Interestingly, as the Austin police chief confirmed afterward, students and other civilians responsibly pulled rifles from their cars and fired back at Whitman in an effort to aid the police.

The most infamous event of guns and lawlessness in Texas, however, was the murder of President John F. Kennedy in Dallas in 1963. Kennedy had traveled to Texas to speak to members of the Democratic party. Lee Harvey Oswald, an alienated former marine, shot the President with a high-powered rifle from the sixth floor of a downtown building while Kennedy was riding in a motorcade on his way to make a speech. Afterward, Oswald killed a policeman and the police arrested him. In turn, Jack Ruby, a local saloon owner, shot

and killed Oswald to avenge Kennedy's death. Critics blamed the loose gun laws and the Texas frontier heritage for this tragic incident. Today most reasonable people realize, however, that guns and violence are a national problem and that it was wrong to blame a state for this terrible event.

The tragic events in Dallas were broadcast live to the nation on television, which provided unprecedented coverage of breaking news. Television was a technology that had reached the popular market after World War II. WBAP-TV in Fort Worth in 1948 was the first station in Texas. It was quickly followed by others, until by 1985 there were 76 stations, and almost every home possessed a television set. The stations provided information, ideas, and entertainment comparable in importance to the "telegraphic intelligence" of an earlier period. Influenced by outside events that further lessened its isolation, Texas continued its change in remarkable ways. One of the most important was the end of segregation.

The National Association for the Advancement of Colored People (NAACP) had been suppressed by the Ku Klux Klan in the 1920s, but after the Klan fell apart in the 1930s because of internal organizational problems and outside resistance, the NAACP revived. Its purpose was to win equality for African Americans, and in 1944

These protesters marched in 1963 in San Antonio to show their support for a desegregation ordinance.

It took a Supreme Court decision to enable Herman Marion Sweatt to enroll at the previously all-white University of Texas Law School in 1950.

it scored a key victory in the U.S. Supreme Court in a case that originated in Texas. In 1940, Lonnie Smith, a black dentist from Houston, although eligible to vote, was denied the right to participate in the Democratic party primary election because of his race. With the aid of the NAACP he brought suit, *Smith* v. *Allwright,* against the Democratic party, claiming violation of the 14th and 15th Amendments of the U.S. Constitution. The 15th Amendment made illegal any denial of suffrage, the right to vote, because of race; the 14th Amendment prevented any state intervention in the voting process.

The Texas Democratic party argued that the amendments did not apply to it because it was a private organization and Smith could vote in the general election. The primary, however, selected party candidates for office. Since only white people were allowed to vote in the primary and because the Democrats dominated state politics, the U.S. Supreme Court declared in 1944 that African Americans had been "indirectly denied" the right to vote. The court thus declared the "white primary"

illegal, and after that blacks began to participate in primary elections.

From 1945 to 1956 the NAACP, in addition, brought court cases to end inequality in the schools. For example, the association protested the deplorable situation at Moshier Valley, a town near Fort Worth, where the black school had no lights, no heat, and no water. At La Grange, near Houston, three grades were mixed in one room and the black teachers also had to work as janitors.

In addition, the NAACP supported the effort of Herman Marion Sweatt, a postal worker from Houston who wanted to become a lawyer. Sweatt applied to the University of Texas Law School in 1946. The school would not admit him because he was black, and set up a law school for blacks at Texas Southern University in Houston. It was thought by state politicians that the new law school would meet the "separate but equal" test of the 1896 Supreme Court ruling in *Plessy* v. *Ferguson*. Sweatt objected, however, and with the help of the NAACP argued in the case *Sweatt* v. *Painter* that the schools were not comparable in faculty, tradition, or facilities. Indeed, the new school was located in a basement. The United States Supreme Court agreed and ruled in favor of Sweatt's admission to the University of Texas in 1950. This was a clear rejection of the "separate but equal" doctrine, which supported segregation.

Shortly thereafter, in 1954, the famous Supreme Court case of *Brown* v. *Board of Education of Topeka* banned segregation in public schools. The justices ruled that separate schools were by their very nature

unequal. Usually the black schools had the worst teachers, worst books, and worst buildings. The Supreme Court, therefore, ended the old doctrine of "separate but equal" and demanded racial integration of the schools.

Integration in regular college classes in Texas had actually started earlier, at Del Mar College in Corpus Christi in 1952. It was followed by other colleges, including, in 1964, Rice University, which had been set up for white students only. In 1965 Jerry LeVias broke the color line in Texas college sports when he played football for Southern Methodist University and won All-American honors in 1968. After witnessing his talent, other schools and coaches began to recruit blacks for their athletic teams.

The NAACP, meanwhile, met resistance as it pushed for integration of the elementary and secondary schools. School boards in Rusk and La Grange fired black teachers who favored integration. In Sulphur Springs a black teacher who spoke for integration was told to move away. Pistol shots and shotgun blasts from unidentified assailants ripped through his home to make sure the warning was heard. Governor Allen Shivers, in office since 1950, won reelection in 1954 on his promise to oppose integration. Texas Rangers were sent to hinder the efforts of black students to enter previously all-white schools in Mansfield and Texarkana. After the mid-1950s, however, following strong support for integration by the federal government—soldiers escorted black students to Central High School in Little Rock, Arkansas, in 1957, for instance—resistance in Texas declined.

In 1955, 66 school districts out of the 1,900 in Texas began to integrate—including those in Austin, San Antonio, San Angelo, El Paso, and Corpus Christi. More than 120 districts had begun the process by 1957, but court orders were needed to start to integrate Dallas and Houston in 1960. By 1970 all institutions of higher education had integrated, and all school districts had either begun or completed the process. School integration was no longer a point of issue with most Texas politicians or citizens.

Integration, meanwhile, touched other parts of Texas society. In 1950 in Houston five African Americans, arguing that their taxes helped to support the municipal golf course, filed a suit to use it, and won. In Galveston a group of blacks simply went out and began to play. The greenskeeper did not argue, but simply came out and collected a fee. Through protests and action, blacks integrated beaches, lunch counters, restaurants, and theaters throughout the state. Separate drinking fountains, restrooms, and waiting rooms disappeared as a greater tolerance emerged.

The old "Jim Crow" laws crumbled under the assault of the 1950s and 1960s.

Students at an integrated school in San Antonio in 1955. Since it had long had a mixed population, San Antonio, of the large cities, reacted most calmly to the new integration laws.

Blacks and whites are both served at a San Antonio cafeteria in 1960. In the 1950s and 1960s, the last remaining Jim Crow laws were abolished.

The headline of the San Antonio Express *announces the start of the drive to integrate the city's lunch counters in March 1960.*

This was because of the courage of the protestors and because of the sense of decency among others. All over the state there were small meetings to discuss what, morally, was the right thing to do. In Galveston, for example, the white owners of retail stores met to decide what to do about blacks who wanted to be served like other people at the lunch counters. There was fear that if a business served black customers the white ones would go away.

George Clampett, a pharmacist in Galveston, stood up and told his group about a conversation with his partner. "You know, Grady and I got together and discussed this business about losing business, causing trouble, and we finally got around to the ultimate question—what is right?" They concluded that if blacks could buy Kleenex and toothpaste, they could also buy hamburgers and Cokes. That was what was just, and as it turned out the business owners' fears were exaggerated. The pharmacists, for example, lost only one white customer, and she returned in a week.

With no black in the state leglislature or as a member of Congress in 1961, the NAACP also encouraged the political activity of the African-American community. As a result, by 1985 there were 14 blacks in the legislature and one in the U.S. Congress. During this time, Houstonians elected Barbara Jordan, an African American, to the state senate, where she served from 1967 to 1971, and then to the U.S. House of Representatives, where she represented Houston from 1972 to 1978.

Mexican Americans followed the lead of African Americans in seeking civil rights. The state's Hispanic population had dropped to a low of 4 percent in 1887, but with the possibility of finding better jobs Mexicans began moving northward after 1890. There were no border restrictions until 1917, and even after that Mexicans simply waded across the Rio Grande and entered the country illegally. Crossings slowed during the Great Depression and then increased during World War II with the return of good jobs. By 1990 about one-fourth of the population was Hispanic. This was twice the number of African Americans in the state. The rest were white, about 60 percent, with a small number of recent immigrants from Asia.

As might be expected from the geography, the largest number of Mexican Americans lived in South and West Texas. They provided most of the cheap labor, especially in farming areas, where some of the old racial prejudice lingered. In the cities there was also some difficulty, but rich Hispanics had little trouble integrating into white neighborhoods. Like African Americans, however, most Mexican Americans lived a separate life. There were separate schools, churches, shops, living areas, and holidays. Barrios, poor Mexican districts in cities, developed in South Texas.

Various political organizations tried to

unite and help the Hispanics. The League of United Latin American Citizens (LULAC) started in 1929; the Political Association of Spanish-Speaking Organizations (PASO) began in 1961; the Mexican-American Youth Organization (MAYO) organized in 1967; and La Raza Unida started in 1970. These groups often had the same goals, but differed in style and action. At Crystal City, a small town southwest of San Antonio, in 1963, for example, PASO worked with the Teamsters Union to organize the Mexican-American workers at the Del Monte canning factory. In the process, the population, which was 80 percent Hispanic, rallied and swept the Anglo elite out of the city council, where they had ruled since the founding of the town in 1907. After competing efforts by MAYO and La Raza Unida in the town, there have been various compromises with the whites but no more exclusion of the Mexican Americans from political power.

Some outstanding Hispanic political leaders also emerged. Henry B. González served on the San Antonio city council and then in the Texas legislature. He was noted for his stand against segregation. In the Texas Senate in 1957, for example, he spoke for 36 hours to oppose such a bill. He became a U.S. congressman in 1961 with a vow to fight for low-cost housing and civil rights. Proud of his heritage, González once commented, "There is no greater tribute than to be an American. There is no greater compliment than to be called an American of Mexican descent."

Henry G. Cisneros, another outstanding Mexican-American politician, was a successful mayor of San Antonio in the 1980s

Barbara Jordan: I Have No Fear

During the depression year of 1936 Barbara Jordan, the youngest of three daughters, was born in Houston to a poor African-American family. Her parents believed in the value of education; when she returned from school with a report card of five A's and a B, her father would ask, "Why do you have a B?" She went to Texas Southern University, graduated in 1956, and then enrolled in the Boston University Law School. She was the only woman in a class of 128, graduated in 1959, and returned to Houston to set up a private law practice that started on her family's dining room table.

Determined to help people in poverty, Jordan ran for election to the Texas House of Representatives. She lost twice, in 1962 and 1964, but then in 1966 after redistricting in Houston, she won a seat to the Texas Senate. She was the first black woman to ever gain such a position. When asked if she were scared, she said, "I have a tremendous amount of faith in my own capacity. I know how to read and write and think, so I have no fear."

After establishing a reputation for cogent speaking and patient work, Jordan was elected again to the Texas Senate in 1968 and then from 1972 to 1978 served as a member of the U.S. Congress. Jordan was the first black woman from Texas or the South in the House of Representatives, and former President Lyndon Johnson helped gain her appointment to the House Judiciary Committee. There she gained national attention in 1974 for the investigation and condemnation of the actions of President Richard Nixon in the Watergate scandal. "We, the people?" she asked during the impeachment resolutions. "I felt for many years that somehow George Washington and Alexander Hamilton just left me out by mistake. But through the process of amendment, interpretation, and court decision, I have finally been included in 'We, the people.' My faith in the Constitution is whole, it is complete, it is total. I am not going to sit here and be an idle spectator to the diminution, the subversion, and the destruction of the Constitution."

Two years later Jordan was chosen as the keynote speaker for the Democratic National Convention in New York, which was a tribute not only to her own accomplishments but also to the potential of African Americans in politics. Jordan said, however, that she had little desire to become a long-term politician and chose not to run for reelection in 1978. She returned to Texas to become a professor at the LBJ School of Public Affairs at the University of Texas at Austin.

When San Antonio voters elected Henry G. Cisneros mayor in 1981, he became the first Hispanic mayor of a major U.S city.

and then became secretary of the Department of Housing and Urban Development for the Clinton administration in 1993. As a measure of increasing political participation, in 1980 there were approximately 1,000 Mexican Americans in various political positions in Texas; by 1986 this number had increased to 1,600. In 1980, moreover, 10 percent of the legislature was Hispanic; in 1994 the number was 13 percent.

The strong influx of Mexicans who crossed the border without permission in the 1960s and 1970s created both a benefit and a problem. Texas businessmen liked Mexican labor because it was cheap and reliable—particularly good for harvesting crops, unskilled factory work, lawn service, food service jobs, construction, and house painting. The problem came with providing services for illegal aliens. It became a court case for the Houston schools: Was it necessary to educate the children of illegal immigrants free of charge? The Texas legislature had said no in 1975, but Judge Woodrow Seals of the U.S. District Court

ruled for free education in 1977. He did not deny the extra tax burden created by these children, but without education, he said, the cities would have a dependent subclass of people roaming the streets. "Children," he wrote, "are the basic resource of our society." Schools thus had to educate all the children who came to their doors.

In the 20th century the state has spent almost half its income on education—no other segment of the state budget has taken so much money or attracted so much attention. In 1949 laws sponsored by Representative Claude Gilmer and Senator A. M. Aiken mandated a school year of nine months, minimum standards for teachers, and larger amounts of state support, especially for poor districts. The Gilmer-Aiken laws soon brought improvement in the schools, yet arguments about school funding and competence continued over the next several decades. All the governors since the 1950s have campaigned with a promise of "no new taxes," despite obvious school funding problems and one of the lowest tax rates in the nation (ranked 41st out of 50 states in 1986). A report by the U.S. Secretary of Education in 1982 revealed that Texas ranked 42nd in the percentage of students who graduated from high school, and below national averages in test scores, teacher–pupil ratios, and teacher salaries.

Governor Mark White, who served from 1983 to 1987, responded to the negative report by appointing a special committee on public education to make suggestions for change. Headed by H. Ross Perot, a Dallas millionaire, the committee presented a report that became the basis for the

Educational Reform Act of 1984. The law provided better salaries for teachers, competency testing of students, and a "no pass, no play" rule, which meant students had to pass their classes with a grade average of 70 percent in order to participate in extracurricular activities, particularly sports. The new rule brought nationwide attention, irritation to those Texans who loved sports, and a certain fame to Perot, who went on to become an independent candidate for President of the United States in 1992. The increased funding for the schools, however, was frustrated by a failing economy in Texas, a major factor in the defeat of Governor White in the 1986 election.

Meanwhile, there were significant changes in the political makeup of the state. Since the time of Sam Houston, most Texans had been loyal to the Democratic party. But in 1952 Texans crossed party lines to vote for Dwight D. Eisenhower for President. He was a member of the Republican party, but he promised to give Texas control over its tidelands, including the continental shelf, which reaches six miles out into the Gulf of Mexico. The tidelands were important because they contained petroleum deposits. The Republican party also got a boost from the election of John Tower to the U.S. Senate. In 1960 Lyndon B. Johnson, a Democrat, became Vice President and gave up his Senate position. Tower, a Republican, ran for Johnson's empty seat and won.

Inspired by Tower's victory, some of the more conservative Democrats—those who wished to keep Texas as it was—switched parties and became Republicans. John Connally, a friend of Lyndon Johnson and a conservative Democrat, was one of those. He was governor of Texas from 1963 to 1969 and was wounded when President John F. Kennedy was killed in Dallas. As governor, Connally gave support to business and higher education and held control of the party for conservative Democrats. During the early 1970s, however, Connally, who had Presidential ambitions, became a Republican. Although all the governors after Connally tended to be fiscally conservative, these changes meant that Texas now became a two-party state like much of the rest of the country.

In 1972, for example, Democrat Dolph Briscoe barely won election as governor over Republican Henry Grover after a banking scandal had damaged the leadership of the Democrats. Briscoe remained in office until 1979 when William Clements, a Republican, was able to win the governor's race. Clements was defeated by Mark White, a Democrat, in 1982, but returned by defeating White in 1986.

In 1990 Democrat Ann W. Richards, the state treasurer, defeated Republican millionaire Clayton Williams. She had gained national recognition in 1988 after delivering a rousing keynote speech at the Democratic National Convention. Richards was the second woman elected governor in Texas history, the first being Miriam "Ma" Ferguson in 1924. In addition, Kay Bailey Hutchison, a Republican from Dallas, defeated Nikki Van Hightower, a Houston Democrat, for state treasurer. Two years later, Hutchison won a U.S. Senate seat. Her election gave Texas two Republican senators—the other being Phil Gramm, a conservative Democrat-turned-Republi-

Dallas billionaire Ross Perot achieved national prominence in 1992 when he staged an unsuccessful run for the Presidency. In this book he outlined his commonsense ideas of how government should be run.

The 1991 inauguration of Ann W. Richards as governor of Texas. She advocated a "New Texas," with good schools, freedom from crime, and quality health care. According to one journalist, "a sense of fun, irreverence, and general cussedness" are her defining characteristics.

participation for minorities and women, commented at the time:

> Three kinds of words cover the needs of a woman who wants to make it in politics. The first is "awareness." Look at the facts of the status of women and women in politics. The second word is "assertiveness" because it means aggression; the word "aggression" tends to strike fear in the hearts of men. The third word is "audacity" . . . even members of my family flinched when I thought of running for governor.

While politics at the state and local level churned with the changes brought by women, minorities, and the development of the Republican party, Texans also revealed extraordinary strength at the national level. The death of John F. Kennedy in 1963 made Lyndon B. Johnson President of the United States, the first Texan to attain that high office. All his life he had dedicated himself to politics; he had been a congressman from 1937 to 1949 and a senator from 1949 to 1961.

He won election over Coke Stevenson in a runoff for the Democratic primary for the Senate in 1948 by the slim margin of 87 votes of a total of more than 1 million votes cast. There were objections about fraudulent voting from both sides, but the election held and Johnson jokingly called himself "Landslide Lyndon." He easily beat his Republican opponent in the general election by a margin of two to one.

Johnson moved rapidly into a position of leadership in the Senate—party whip (the number two party leader) in 1951, minority leader in 1953, and majority leader in 1954.

can. Richards, however, was reelected governor.

The success of these women in the 1990s shows the impact of women's increasing role in Texas politics. About 18 percent of the members of the 1994 legislature were women—up from 5 percent in 1985. This surge can be traced in Texas to the establishment of local chapters of the National Organization of Women in 1966 and an unsuccessful, but impressive, race for the Democratic nomination for governor in 1972 by Frances "Sissy" Farenthold, a lawyer from Corpus Christi. Farenthold, a liberal who wanted to gain wider political

Vice President Lyndon B. Johnson (far right) listens to President John F. Kennedy speak in Fort Worth on November 22, 1963. Kennedy was assassinated in Dallas later that day.

He developed persuasive techniques that utilized not only his profound knowledge of politics but also his intimidating size: Johnson was 6 feet, 3 inches tall and weighed 230 pounds. As he talked he would back people into a corner, lean into their face, tap them on the chest, and grab the lapels of men's suits. The "Johnson Treatment," as the technique was known, was effective, and Johnson often got his way. At the same time, however, he knew how to compromise and to give others what they needed.

Johnson's dream as President was to create a "Great Society." He wanted to end poverty, improve city living, extend civil rights, and improve education. It is strange that empathy for the issues of civil rights and urban problems would come from a person who was part southerner and part westerner, but Johnson saw himself destined to complete the New Deal reforms of his early mentor President Franklin D. Roosevelt.

With his considerable political knowledge Johnson was able to complete the domestic program of his predecessor, President Kennedy, and add legislation of his own. He obtained passage of the Civil Rights Act of 1964, which outlawed racial discrimination in public places and gender discrimination in the workplace. This was one of the great reform laws of the century, which not only helped to end segregation but also enhanced social equality. The Economic Opportunity Act of 1964 provided job training programs, loans for rural families and small business, and aid for migrant workers. This act was a part of the War on Poverty, a program started by President Kennedy. The energy Johnson injected into government helped carry him to a crushing victory over Republican candidate Barry Goldwater of Arizona in the 1964 Presidential election.

Over the next several years Johnson got Congress to pass legislation for increased funding of elementary and secondary education; Medicare, a program of medical insurance for the aged; the Voting Rights Act of 1965, which protected black voters; a "model cities" program to improve safety, parks, and transportation; and a beautification program inspired by his wife, Lady Bird Johnson, to remove junkyards from sight, reduce the size and number of billboards, and provide landscaping along the national highways.

Money for the dream, however, drained off to fight the war in Vietnam that had started before Johnson became President. Unable to win the war, Johnson retired from politics in 1968 to his hill country ranch near Austin. Texans voted for Richard M. Nixon, the Republican candidate in 1968, and for Jimmy Carter, a Democrat, in 1976. In the 1980s Texans supported Republicans Ronald Reagan and George Bush. Bush had made his fortune in Texas oil and claimed Texas as his home state. He was elected President in 1988 and Texans voted for Bush again in 1992 when Bill Clinton, a Democrat, won the Presidency.

The influence of these national politicians ensured that Texas would receive its share of federal investments, such as Fort Hood at Killeen and Lackland Air Force

The "Johnson Treatment" in action. Johnson's powers of persuasion were legendary.

President Johnson speaks with a member of the Job Corps, one of his Great Society programs that was created to help inner-city teenagers gain practical work experience.

Two former governors of Texas, Price Daniel (left) and John Connally, greet each other at the inauguration of Governor Bill Clements in 1979. George Bush, a sometime Houstonian and future U.S. President, smiles in the background.

Base in San Antonio. One of the most impressive was the Lyndon B. Johnson Manned Spacecraft Center. When John F. Kennedy became President he promised that an American astronaut would step on the surface of the moon within 10 years. As a part of this effort, the National Aeronautics and Space Administration (NASA) built a control center south of Houston. As Vice President, Johnson, along with Congressman Albert Thomas of Houston, facilitated the selection of that site. In five years the center employed 5,000 people, and engineers at the headquarters directed the

successful launch of *Apollo 11* in 1969. From the surface of the moon Astronaut Neil Armstrong said to the world, "Houston . . . Tranquility Base here. The *Eagle* has landed!"

This was a triumph for the United States that Texas could share, and there were others. Monroe D. Anderson, a rich cotton merchant, died in 1939 and gave most of his fortune—about $20 million—to a charity organization, the M. D. Anderson Foundation. He wanted it spent to advance medical knowledge and to relieve human suffering. The foundation decided to start the Texas Medical Center in Houston, which over time included 50 buildings on 500 acres south of downtown. The buildings include the Baylor Medical School, Texas Dental School, Arabia Temple Crippled Children's Clinic, Texas Children's Hospital, M. D. Anderson Cancer Center, University of Houston School of Nursing, and a half dozen other hospitals. At the center Drs. Michael E. DeBakey and Denton Cooley began their famous heart transplant operations while the Cancer Center became one of the best hospitals of its kind. The importance of the Texas Medical Center is underscored by the fact that it is the single largest employer in Houston, a city that is the fourth largest in the country.

Another accomplishment for Texas, perhaps less sensational and awe-inspiring but nonetheless important for the state and the nation, is the art interest of John and Dominique de Menil, who were French refugees from World War II. John de Menil was chairman of the executive committe of Schlumberger, an oil tool manufacturer in Houston. They collected contemporary art and, in 1971, paid for the Rothko Chapel

An Apollo *astronaut performs a lunar training exercise at the Lyndon B. Johnson Manned Spacecraft Center in Houston.*

Dr. Michael E. DeBakey performs heart surgery at the Methodist Hospital in the Texas Medical Center in Houston. Iron Mike has performed more than 40,000 heart operations.

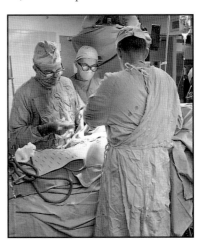

Iron Mike

Michael E. DeBakey, M.D., was born in Lake Charles, Louisiana, in 1908. His father ran a drugstore and DeBakey became interested in medicine. He attended Tulane Medical School and in 1948 joined Baylor Medical School in the Texas Medical Center as professor of surgery. He became the country's best-known doctor for heart disease and a pioneer in heart transplants. By 1981 he had performed 40,000 heart operations of all kinds.

He maintained a rigorous schedule. He went to bed at midnight, got up at 4:00 in the morning, and then performed about 10 operations during the day. He never took a vacation and worked every day of the week. Iron Mike, as he was called, was a perfectionist. He tried to do everything right because in heart surgery even a small mistake can kill the patient. He said about his medical students, "I try to teach them to strive for excellence in their work. . . . You know, everybody can do better than they think they can if they'd try. They must learn to be precise— precise in their thinking, precise in their language, precise in their work."

on the campus of the University of St. Thomas in Houston. The small brick building contains 14 huge dark paintings by the postexpressionist artist Mark Rothko. Outside, in a small reflecting pool, the de Menils placed a sculpture by Barnett Newman. It is a large four-sided steel shaft balanced on a pyramid point, called *The Broken Obelisk* in honor of civil rights leader Martin Luther King, Jr. Travelers from around the world have sought the chapel as a special place for quiet thought and peace.

After her husband's death, Dominique de Menil built a museum in Houston to house her 10,000 pieces of art. Other world cities had tried to obtain her collection, but she kept it in Texas. At the opening of her gallery and museum in 1987, she said,

"Artists are economically useless—yet they are indispensable. A political regime where artists are persecuted is stifling, unbearable. Man cannot live by bread alone. We need painters, poets, musicians, filmmakers, philosophers, dancers, and saints."

Both Houston and Dallas in the 1970s and 1980s built stunning skylines, a dazzling outline of buildings across the horizon. The world's best architects designed the structures. In Houston, for example, in 1972–73 Philip Johnson of New York put up Pennzoil Place, twin black towers in the shape of glass trapezoids. For Dallas, I. M. Pei of New York created a reverse-tiered city hall, resembling an inverted pyramid, in 1978. The British sculptor Henry Moore was commissioned to create a large bronze

Astrodome

The Harris County Domed Stadium, or Astrodome, was the first enclosed, air-conditioned sports arena large enough for either baseball or football games. The dome was 710 feet across and 218 feet high. A batted baseball could not hit the roof. The stadium could seat 45,000 for baseball and 52,000 for football.

When the Astrodome opened in 1965, there was a problem with lighting. In daylight the glare from the transparent ceiling and its supporting steel girders was so bright that baseball players could not see high fly balls. They wore their batting helmets in the field to protect their heads and tried playing, unsuccessfully, with different colored balls. The problem was solved by painting the plastic sheets of the roof.

Then the grass died because it did not get enough sunlight. This second problem was solved by putting down a carpet of artificial grass called Astroturf, manufactured just for the Astrodome by a company called Chemstrand. Since then, Astroturf has been used in both indoor and outdoor stadiums. It is easier to care for than grass but has been blamed for an increasing number of sports injuries.

The Houston Astrodome is home to two professional sports teams, baseball's Houston Astros and the Houston Oilers of the National Football League.

in front of the city hall called *Dallas Piece*. To celebrate its 250th birthday in 1968 San Antonio put up the soaring Tower of the Americas.

The building that created the most discussion, however, was the Houston Astrodome. It was promoted by Judge Roy Hofheinz and R. E. "Bob" Smith, who had acquired a major league baseball franchise. They needed a stadium. Houston air was hot, humid, and buzzing with mosquitoes, so Hofheinz had the idea of a covered, air-conditioned arena. Engineers said that such a building could be constructed, although it had never been done before—certainly not a stadium large enough to cover a baseball field.

Harris County voters granted the money and in 1965 the Astrodome opened. It was large enough to enclose the entire field and high enough so that no ball could hit the roof. At the first game the Houston Astros beat the New York Yankees 2 to 1, even though Mickey Mantle hit a home run. When that happened the huge scoreboard, the first of its kind, flashed, "Tilt!" The Astrodome was a national sports sensation,

and other cities copied the idea. The gentle curve of domed stadiums has transformed the look of urban skylines, and its artificial playing surface, Astroturf, has changed the technology of field sports.

The new stadium also signified the beginning of major league professional sports in Texas, a measurement of urban maturity. Whether reasonable or not, there is a common idea that for a city or state to be counted as worthwhile, or "big league," it must support a major league professional sports team. The Houston Astros started in 1962 as the Colt 45s but changed their name two years later. The Texas Rangers began to play baseball in Arlington, between Dallas and Fort Worth, in 1972. Professional basketball started with the San Antonio Spurs in 1967. The Houston Rockets opened basketball play in 1971, as did the Dallas Mavericks in 1980.

If it can be said that Texas has a favorite sport, however, it is football. Large linemen, smart quarterbacks, lean runners, prancing bands, nimble cheerleaders, worried coaches, yelling fans—these make up a fall weekend in Texas. Small towns paint

Dominique de Menil hired Italian architect Renzo Piano to build a museum to house her vast collection of modern art. She is shown seated in front of a painting by Max Ernst, Return of The Beautiful Gardener.

the schedule of their high school team on billboards. Big towns follow college "shoot-outs."

Sports act as a mirror of a society, and in Texas, football is a reflection of the old Texas myth. Men and boys play the game, while women and girls sit on the sidelines and cheer. There have been a few exceptions. In 1948, for example, the coach at Stinnett High School noticed Frankie Groves at a school picnic. She was 16 years old, 105 pounds, and a vicious tackler. The coach let her play in the school homecoming game. Frankie said afterward, "They weren't so tough. Heck, I didn't even get my lipstick smeared." In short order, however, the high schools ruled that girls could not play. The game was reserved for boys, although in the mid-1990s that rule was again challenged.

One of the greatest Texas players was "Slinging Sammy" Baugh. Born in Temple, he learned to throw the football with a sidearm motion. He went to Texas Christian University in the 1930s and taught the Southwest Conference the importance of the pass play. During a game against the University of Texas, the TCU center told the Texas players, "Gentlemen, Mr. Baugh is going to pass again. I don't know just where it'll go, but it'll be good. Ready?" The completed pass gained 25 yards. Baugh went on to play for the Washington Redskins from 1937 to 1952, and his success is one of the main reasons professional teams use the pass play so much today.

The Dallas Cowboys and the Houston Oilers began their professional football life in 1960. The Oilers won their first years,

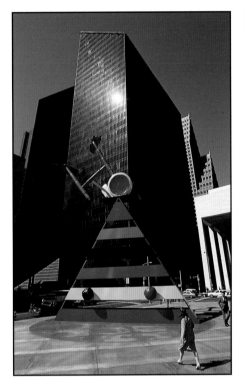

then lost for several years, and won again under Coach "Bum" Phillips. He wore western boots and hats to the games, and had the humor of a West Texas cowboy. He said about playing the Pittsburgh Steelers, "When we play them, it's not a game—it's a collision. The team with the most Band-Aids wins."

The Cowboys rose to greatness with Coach Tom Landry. Under Landry the team twice won the Super Bowl, in 1972 and 1978, and then twice more with coach Jimmy Johnson, in 1993 and 1994. The Cowboys began playing their games in Arlington in 1971, and on television the players won a national following with their "shotgun" formation. This play, designed specifically for passing, featured the quarterback standing five yards back and

These two buildings are vivid displays of the dazzling architecture that was built in Houston in the 1970s and 1980s. Houston also maintains notable works of public art including these sculptures by Juan Miro (left), and David Addicks.

receiving a hike of the ball from the center. In the 1980s the Cowboys became known as "America's Team."

Football tends to be a male sport because of the need for heavy, strong players. Texas, however, produced one of the best female athletes in the history of athletics. "Babe" Didrikson was born in Port Arthur in 1914 and grew up in Beaumont. She loved sports and practiced running hurdles by jumping over the neighbors' hedges. While playing sandlot baseball, she hit so many home runs that her friends called her "Babe" after the famous professional player Babe Ruth.

In 1932 she won the team championship by herself at the Amateur Athletic Union (AAU) track championships and the same year went to the Olympics, where she set two world records. In 1935 she began to play golf, and between 1940 and 1950 she won every major women's golf title. Didrikson married professional wrestler George Zaharias in 1938. She said she found him attractive because he was the only man she had ever met who could drive a golf ball farther than she could. In 1953 she was diagnosed with cancer, but she continued to play for the benefit of cancer research. She died in 1956. Newspaper writers selected Babe Didrikson Zaharias as the best woman athlete of the first half of the century.

The number of women athletes has increased in Texas and elsewhere in the country since the 1970s. Title IX, which is a part of the 1972 federal Education Act, gave females an equal chance to play sports. People realized that women and girls can become fine athletes. In recent years, for example, the Lady Longhorns of the University of Texas have performed with championship excellence in swimming and basketball.

Though Texas can feel pride in its art, architecture, music, literature, and sports, it is still faced with problems. Many of these difficulties are common everywhere in American life—traffic congestion and pollution, for example. Covering the state is a network of modern roads, highways, and freeways, a vast improvement over the stump-strewn dirt ruts of the 19th century. Texas is first in the nation in miles (300,000) of roads. Texans have taken to automobiles like Comanches to horses. There are more than 14 million licensed motor vehicles, cars, trucks, and motorcycles in Texas today—more than one vehicle per adult driver. It all adds up to a lot of traffic, especially in the cities.

The busiest freeway in the state in 1993 was Interstate Highway 635, which loops around the north side of Dallas and carried 248,000 vehicles per day. In Houston, U.S. 59 carried 238,000 vehicles per day. These compare to the busiest road in America, the Santa Monica Freeway in Los Angeles, which takes 300,000 vehicles per day. The result of all this traffic is that accidents and traffic jams and air pollution have become a daily part of life in major Texas cities.

Coach Tom Landry of the Dallas Cowboys confers on the sidelines with quarterback Roger Staubach. The machinelike efficiency of the team and the cool demeanor of the coach provided a model for the teams of the 1980s.

Industries have added to the air pollution as well. As early as 1940, people in Houston complained of foul-smelling air, and in 1958 airplane pilots could find their way from Dallas to Houston by following a one-mile-wide plume of haze streaking northward. For Houston the problem was worse when an east wind collected the industrial pollutants from the ship channel and blew them into the city. The sulphur content of the air was high enough to darken the color of paint and kill plants. Houston recently ranked second in the nation in terms of ozone pollution, but to a lesser degree Dallas and the other large cities suffered from the same problem.

In addition, there has been water pollution, and the worst offender has been the Houston Ship Channel. In the 1940s it became the receptacle for all sorts of wastes—chemicals, grease, and sewage. No fish were able to live in it, and when heavy rains flushed the channel into Galveston Bay there were massive fish kills. In 1967 a member of the Federal Water Control Administration said, "The Houston Ship Channel, in all frankness, is one of the worst polluted bodies of water in the nation. In fact, on almost any day this channel may be the most badly polluted body of water in the entire world. Most days it would top the list."

In the early 1970s Houston and its industries began a program to clean up the waterway. By 1972, 18 species of water life had returned; by 1975 there were 34. In 1980 fish were seen in the turning basin. It was a clear victory that showed that such programs could succeed and that human beings could clean up their own mess if they wished to do so.

There was yet another kind of pollution Texas had to deal with—garbage. Throughout Texas before 1968, people burned their garbage. In Galveston, for example, the dump continually smoldered and left a smoky plume to mark the way for tourists going to the island for a holiday. After the state banned burning, towns and cities began using landfills. This kind of disposal merely buried the garbage and trash under loads of dirt where it was hoped it would rot away and do no damage. Garbage accumulation, however, raised unresolved questions about hazardous wastes, such as old paint, and also about the location of dumps. No one wanted to live next door to a garbage dump. As Mayor Louie Welch of Houston once said, "You know, when it comes to garbage, people want us to pick it up, but they don't want us to put it down again, especially if it is near their house."

These problems of pollution and traffic have become worse as the cities and population have grown. From 1950 to 1990 the population of the state leaped from about 7 to 17 million people. With 8 of every 10 living inside city limits, Texas passed the national average. In 1990 Houston became the fourth largest city in the United States, after New York, Los Angeles, and Chicago.

In rankings of metropolitan areas, Houston plus its close neighbors, Dallas-Fort

In 1967, the Houston Ship Channel was considered one of the most polluted bodies of water in the nation. In the 1970s, however, Houston established programs to clean up the channel.

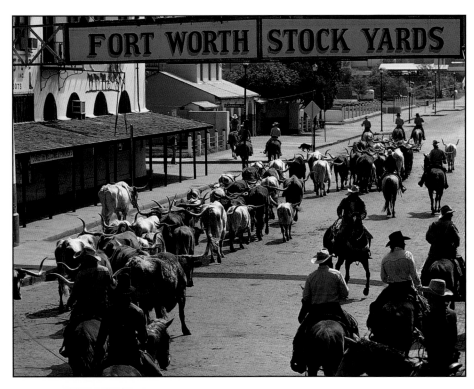

FORT WORTH STOCK YARDS

This ceremonial drive of longhorns into the stockyards commemorates the "Cowtown" heritage of Fort Worth. The historic stockyards are now mainly a tourist area, with shops, restaurants, and one of the largest western dance halls in Texas.

West Texas oil rigs at work. Falling oil prices in the 1980s sent the Texas economy into a depression, and there was only a partial recovery in the 1990s. A joke of the time asked: "How do you get a Texas oilman out of the tree?" The grim answer was, "Cut the rope."

Worth, ranked ninth in the nation in 1990; Houston-Galveston was tenth. In 1990 only a little over 1 percent of the population in Texas consisted of actual working farmers or ranchers. That was a vast difference from the Texas of 1850, when most people, about 90 percent, were involved with farming.

With television sets, radio, newspapers, postal service, paved roads, and cars, everyone was connected to the cities and city life. Farmers became businessmen with their use of machines and scientific farm practices. Cotton remained the most important plant crop in 1990, as it had been for 100 years, but livestock production, especially cattle, was four times more valuable than cotton. Cattle feedlots, large pens to hold and feed cattle, popular in the 1970s and 1980s, have declined, but there was still almost one cow per person in the state in 1990.

A drought from 1950 to 1957 forced farmers to build irrigation systems. They used center-pivot sprinklers that sprinkled giant green circles on the Great Plains, and between 1940 and 1980 they built more than 100 reservoirs. The effort increased water storage 10 times, but there was still a vague worry that someday the water would

run out. Some reservoirs in West Texas have turned salty because of evaporation. Aquifers, moreover, have declined, and some have shown signs of pollution. Without the aquifers or a fresh source of water, West Texas faces a bleak future.

The greatest problem in recent times for Texas, however, has been the oil depression. In the early 1980s about three out of every five businesses in Texas were connected to the oil industry. About one-fourth of the economy was related to petroleum, and thus the state was very sensitive to changes in the world oil markets. Beginning in 1981, the world price of oil began to drop. This was because there was a large amount of petroleum being produced elsewhere in the world, especially in the Middle East. The price declined from $39 per barrel in 1981 to $10 per barrel in 1986. In Texas it takes about $15 per barrel to break even. Above $15 a company can make money; below $15, it takes a loss and may have to go out of business.

As a result of the dropping oil prices, Texas fell into an economic depression. Companies stopped drilling to find petroleum, fired their workers, and sold their equipment. Unemployment rose as high as 17 percent in the Rio Grande Valley and 12

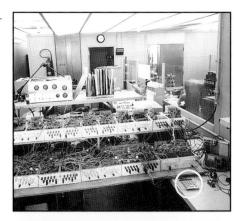

Scientists at Texas Instruments, based in Dallas, invented the world's first hand-held computer.

percent in Houston. People were forced to sell their homes and use up their savings. The savings and loan companies failed, and the state experienced a loss of tax revenues. In 1987 Bob Bullock, the state comptroller, said to the legislature, "The last time [1986] you invited me to speak, you asked me to talk about money. I said at the time that I could make the shortest talk in legislative history: you didn't have any. Today, I would say you have even less."

The oil depression was not as bad as the Great Depression of the 1930s, and some businesses remained healthy. Those involved with communications, aircraft, and electronics helped the rest of the Texas economy. Dallas had more of these types of businesses than Houston did and thus did not suffer as much. Among the more well-known Dallas companies, for example, was Texas Instruments, which had begun producing electronic machines in the 1950s. In 1958 Jack St. Clair Kilby of Texas Instruments invented the integrated circuit, which permitted a reduction in the size of electric instruments. In 1971 it was Kilby who presented to the world the hand calculator, a device that made it easy to add, subtract, multiply, divide, and perform other mathematical functions.

By the late 1980s the oil depression had eased, but it had not completely ended. Other businesses moved to Texas and with the aid of the federal government the worst of the savings and loan crisis passed. The space program continued, and in 1989 the U.S. Department of Energy designated the superconducting supercollider for construction in Texas—at Waxahachie,

In 1986 Texans celebrated the 150th anniversary of their independence from Mexico with this giant cake.

south of Dallas. Work on this expensive scientific atom smasher was suspended, however, in 1993.

In 1986 Texas celebrated its sesquicentennial, the 150th anniversary of its independence from Mexico, with festivities throughout the state. Texas had the third largest population of the states. It was first in the miles of roads and railroads, and first in oil and gas deposits. Its people had made unique contributions to music, medicine, art, literature, sports, politics, and business. There was much to celebrate. Now, in the 1990s, the depression has lessened, the population estimates in 1994 made Texas the second largest state, behind California, and what was celebrated remains as a foundation for the future.

Chronology

9200 B.C.
Paleo-Indians migrate into the Texas Panhandle.

1519
Alonso Alvarez de Piñeda sails along the Texas coast.

1528
Álvar Núñez Cabeza de Vaca becomes shipwrecked on Galveston Island.

1541
Francisco Vásquez de Coronado explores the Southwest and discovers Palo Duro Canyon.

1542
Luis de Moscoso of the de Soto expedition explores East Texas.

1681
Franciscan missionaries establish Ysleta, the oldest surviving settlement in Texas.

1685
La Salle builds Fort St. Louis at Matagorda Bay.

1700
Comanche Indians acquire horses.

1718
Franciscan missionaries establish the Alamo.

1758
San Saba Mission is destroyed by Comanches.

1759
Comanches and their allies defeat Parilla.

1785–86
José de Evia maps the Texas coast.

1821
Jean Laffite is forced to leave Galveston Island.

Jane Long gives birth to the first Anglo-American child in Texas.

First settlers arrive at the Austin land grant.

1835
Texans challenge Mexicans at Gonzales in first battle of the Texas Revolution.

1836
Texas independence is declared.

Battle of the Alamo is won by Santa Anna. All Texan defenders are killed.

James Fannin surrenders at Goliad and 342 Texans are executed.

Sam Houston defeats Santa Anna at the Battle of San Jacinto.

Nine-year-old Cynthia Ann Parker is kidnapped by Comanches.

Augustus C. Allen and John K. Allen found the city of Houston.

Sam Houston is elected first president of the Republic of Texas.

1838
Michael B. Menard founds city of Galveston.

1839
Lone Star Flag is officially adopted by the Republic.

1839
Cherokee Indians are defeated and pushed out of the Republic.

1840
City of Austin is established as the capital.

1842
John Neely Bryan founds Dallas.

1842
Galveston News, the oldest continuing newspaper in Texas, begins publication.

1843
Captured Texans of the Mier expedition are forced to draw for the black bean to determine who will be executed.

1845
Texas joins the United States.

1846
Battles of Palo Alto and Resaca de la Palma begin the war with Mexico.

1849
Fort Worth opens as a military post.

1850
Texas boundaries are redrawn to the present lines as a result of the Compromise of 1850.

Cowboys inside the Equity Bar in Tascosa.

1852

Richard King purchases land for the King Ranch.

1853

The Buffalo Bayou, Brazos and Colorado Railway begins operation as the first Texas railroad.

1854

First telegraph office opens in Marshall.

1860

Cynthia Ann Parker is retaken from the Comanches.

1861

Texas joins the Confederate States of America.

1863

Texans win the Battle of Galveston and the Battle of Sabine Pass.

1865

Civil War ends, freeing all slaves.

1871

Texas A&M University is established.

1875

Quanah Parker and Comanches are defeated.

1876

Voters approve the current state constitution.

1878

Alfred H. Belo sets up the first telephone in Texas between his home and the *Galveston News*.

1881

Voters select Austin as the site of the University of Texas main campus and Galveston for the medical branch.

1887

Texas League is organized for baseball.

1888

Present capitol building is completed in Austin.

1893

First long-distance telephone line is strung between Houston and Galveston.

1894–95

Austin is lighted by 31 towers of electric lights.

1900

Texas ranks sixth in nation for population.

Galveston hurricane kills 6,000 people.

1901

Anthony Lucas discovers oil at Spindletop.

John Henry Kirby forms Kirby Lumber Company, the first multimillion-dollar company in Texas.

1902

Texas Library Association is established.

1914

Houston Ship Channel opens.

1917

Race riot in Houston results in 19 deaths.

Governor James Ferguson is banned from office.

1919

Texas approves the right of women to vote.

1925

Miriam Ferguson becomes the first elected woman governor in the United States.

1930

Dad Joiner discovers the East Texas oil field.

1932

Babe Didrickson wins two gold medals and one silver at the Olympics in Los Angeles.

1935

Walter Prescott Webb publishes *The Texas Rangers*, which helps to establish the Texas myth.

1940

Todd Shipyards on the Houston Ship Channel begins operation in preparation for World War II.

1941-1945

750,000 Texans serve in the military in World War II.

1942

Texas Medical Center opens.

1950

Herman Marion Sweatt is the first black person admitted to the University of Texas Law School.

1958

Jack St. Clair Kilby invents integrated circuits at Texas Instruments in Dallas.

The Buckhorn Saloon, San Antonio.

1960

Dallas Cowboys and Houston Oilers are established as professional football teams.

1961

Johnson Manned Spacecraft Center opens near Houston.

1962

Houston 45s (later Astros) become the first major league baseball team in Texas.

1963

President John F. Kennedy is assassinated in Dallas and Lyndon B. Johnson of Texas becomes President.

1965

Astrodome opens as the world's first air-conditioned stadium for baseball and football.

1969

Neil Armstrong lands on the moon.

1974

Dallas/Fort Worth International Airport opens.

1986

Texas celebrates sesquicentennial birthday.

Oil prices drop to $10 per barrel and Texas suffers oil depression.

1988

George Bush of Houston is elected President of the United States.

1990

Texas ranks third in the nation with a population of 17 million.

Museums and Historic Sites in Texas

Days and times of availability for visitors often change. For the latest general information on sites and museum hours, the most helpful publication is the *Texas State Travel Guide,* printed and distributed free by the Texas Department of Transportation, Division of Travel and Information, P.O. Box 5064, Austin, TX 78763-5064. Tel. 800-452-9292.

Alpine

Museum of the Big Bend
Sul Ross State University
Alpine, TX 79830
Tel. 915-837-8143

Of particular interest are the photographs and artifacts about the Mexican Revolution, ranching, and settlement of the Big Bend region.

Alto

Caddoan Mounds State Historic Site
Alto, TX 75925
Tel. 409-858-3218

This village site of the Caddo Indians includes two ceremonial mounds, a burial mound, a reconstructed house, and an interpretive center.

Austin

Center for American History
Sid Richardson Hall, Unit 2
University of Texas Campus
Austin, TX 78712
Tel. 512-471-5961

Once named the Barker Texas History Center, this library contains the foremost collection of Texana in the state. Along with the Texas State Library, it is used extensively by historians and genealogists. The center presents changing displays of photographs and materials dealing with Texas history.

Elisabet Ney Museum
304 East 44th Street
Austin, TX 78751
Tel. 512-458-2255

One of the state's most renowned artists, Ney created statues that appear in both the Texas State Capitol and in the U.S. Capitol. This museum, a National Historic Site, displays her work at her old studio.

French Legation
802 San Marcos Street
Austin, TX 78702
Tel. 512-472-8180

Built in 1840 by Count Alphonse Dubois de Saligny and now maintained by the State of Texas, the house stands on a secluded bluff overlooking the city. It is the oldest historic house in Austin and the site of the famed "Pig War."

Governor's Mansion
1010 Colorado Street
Austin, TX 78711
Tel. 512-475-2121

Built from 1853 to 1855 by Abner Cook for the leaders of Texas, this white-columned mansion features the well-known painting by Robert Onderdonk, *The Fall of the Alamo,* as well as nails driven into the stair railing by Governor James S. Hogg to prevent his children from sliding down the bannister.

Lyndon B. Johnson Library and Museum
2313 Red River
Austin, TX 78705
Tel. 512-482-5137

The papers of President Johnson are housed in this monumental archives and museum. The first two floors display events of his career. There is also a replica of the Oval Office of the White House in Washington, D.C.

State Capitol
Austin, TX 78711
Tel. 512-475-3037

This is the place to start a historic tour of Texas. The majestic capitol, modeled after the U.S. Capitol in Washington, D.C., dominates 46 acres of aged oak trees and lawn. Although it is the meeting place of the Texas legislature, there are daily guided tours to view the historic flags, statues, and paintings within the statehouse, including William H. Huddle's 1886 painting *The Surrender of Santa Anna.*

State Cemetery
East 7th and Comal Streets
Austin, TX 78711

Some 2,000 famous Texans, including Stephen F. Austin, lie buried here. The white marble grave covering of Albert Sidney Johnston carved by Elisabet Ney is considered one of her best works.

Texas State Library
12th and Brazos Streets
Austin, TX 78711
Tel. 512-475-2445

Located just east of the capitol, the library maintains collections of private papers of prominent Texans for the use of scholars. There is a small exhibit area of historic Texas letters, artifacts from Spanish shipwrecks, and a mural in the lobby by Peter Rogers from which the staring, dark eyes of William B. Travis seem to follow people around the room.

Texas Memorial Museum
2400 Trinity Street
Austin, TX 78705
Tel. 512-471-1604

Exhibits of Texas geology, archaeology, and anthropology can be found here. It is located on the campus of the University of Texas, a block away from the Lyndon B. Johnson Library and the Center for American History.

Beaumont

Babe Didrikson Zaharias Memorial
Gulf Street at I-10
Beaumont, TX 77703
Tel. 713-833-4622

Displayed in one large room are awards, photographs, and newspaper clippings of Babe Didrikson, the best female U.S. athlete of the first half of the 20th century.

Gladys City Boomtown
University Drive and U.S. 69
Beaumont, TX 77710
Tel. 409-835-0823

This reconstruction of nearby oil boomtown Gladys City provides a replica of the village, complete with general store, a surveyor's office, and other buildings.

Texas Energy Museum
600 Main Street
Beaumont, TX 77710
Tel. 409-833-5100

Talking robots and other exhibits at the Energy Museum track the effects of Spindletop and the development of the modern oil industry.

Big Bend

Big Bend National Park
Visitor Center, Panther Junction
Big Bend National Park, TX 79834
Tel. 915-477-2251

There are more than 430 bird species, 1,100 plant types, and several hundred miles of nature trails in this desert park of 801,000 acres. Park rangers present illustrated talks and tours throughout the year. Lady Bird Johnson brought attention to the geologic splendor of this park during her tenure as First Lady with a raft trip down the Rio Grande.

Brownsville

Stillman House Museum
13th Street and Washington
Brownsville, TX 78520
Tel. 512-542-3929

Charles Stillman was a shipowner, merchant, land developer, and a founder of Brownsville. His house, built in 1850, contains family materials, period furnishings, and displays about the history of Brownsville.

Canyon

Palo Duro Canyon State Park
Canyon, TX 79015
Tel. 806-488-2227

Colonel Ranald Mackenzie and his troopers crushed Indian resistance on the southern plains at this site in 1874. Two years later Charles Goodnight established his cattle enterprise in the canyon. Today the historical, musical drama *Texas,* by Paul Green, captures the pioneer spirit. It is presented during the summer months in an amphitheater in the canyon.

Panhandle-Plains Historical Museum
2401 Fourth Avenue
Canyon, TX 79016
Tel. 806-655-7191 or 806-655-7194

This state-supported museum houses more than 1,500,000 items, concentrating on ranching life, oil production, and the Indians of the Panhandle region. Its murals and displays make it one of the best in the state.

Corpus Christi

Centennial House
411 North Broadway
Corpus Christi, TX 78412
Tel. 512-992-6003

Constructed in 1849 of "shellcrete," a type of concrete made with shells, this restored house is the last remaining example from the row of millionaires' mansions that once stood upon this high bluff overlooking the city. It is open to visitors when the flag is flying.

Corpus Christi Museum of Science and History
1900 North Chaparral
Corpus Christi, TX 78401
Tel. 512-883-2862

Although the emphasis is upon natural history, the museum also features an exhibit that displays artifacts from 16th-century wrecks on Padre Island as well as a replica of a Spanish treasure ship.

Heritage Park
1581 North Chaparral
Corpus Christi, TX 78401
Tel. 512-883-0639

Eight turn-of-the-century restored homes in the Old Irishtown section of the city provide a glimpse of Victorian living.

Padre Island National Seashore
9405 South Padre Island Drive
Corpus Christi, TX 78418
Tel. 512-949-8068

The 80-mile center section of Padre Island, 110 miles long, has been preserved in a natural state by the federal government. It is the best unaltered example of the sand barrier islands that run parallel to the Texas coast from Galveston to Port Isabel. Nature trails and tours by park rangers are available.

Texas State Aquarium
2710 North Shoreline Boulevard
Corpus Christi, TX 78463
Tel. 512-886-6018

Exhibits feature the wildlife and fish of the Gulf of Mexico in their various habitats.

U.S.S. *Lexington* Museum on the Bay
2914 North Shoreline Boulevard
Corpus Christi, TX 78402
Tel. 512-888-4873

The Lady Lex, one of the most important aircraft carriers during World War II, now serves as a floating museum that recalls the history of naval aviation and the role of the U.S. Naval Air Station at Corpus Christi. Although not connected to Texas history, nearby at permanent anchor are the replicas of the *Niña, Pinta,* and *Santa Maria* that sailed to the United States from Spain to celebrate the Columbian Quincentennial in 1992.

Dalhart

XIT Museum
108 East Fifth Street
Dalhart, TX 79022
Tel. 806-249-5390

The XIT Ranch, formed in 1885, was one of the most famous in West Texas. This collection emphasizes daily life at the ranch and in the region at the turn of the century.

Dallas

Age of Steam Museum
Fair Park
Washington and Parry
Dallas, TX 75226
Tel. 214-361-6936

Locomotives, trains, Dallas's earliest rail depot, and artifacts from the first part of the 20th century are on display.

Dallas Historical Society
Hall of State
Fair Park
Dallas, TX 75226
Tel. 214-421-5136

This Art Deco building, with murals by Texas artists such as Tom Lea and sculptures of Texas heroes, was built for the Texas Centennial in 1936.

Dallas Museum of Natural History
Fair Park
Second and Grand
Dallas, TX 75226
Tel. 214-421-2169

Exhibits include more than 50 dioramas of Texas wildlife, featuring the plants, animals, and geology of the Southwest.

Old City Park
1717 Gano Street
Dallas, TX 75215
Tel. 214-421-5141

This outstanding collection of structures from 1840 to 1910 represents Dallas and North Texas as they once looked. It includes examples of homes, a city block, a church, a schoolhouse, a farm, and a train depot. It is located in Dallas's earliest city park, where a spring once supplied the town with water.

Sixth Floor Museum
411 Elm Street
Dallas, TX 75202
Tel. 214-653-6666

The point from which Lee Harvey Oswald shot President John F. Kennedy is now a permanent exhibition area dedicated to the life and death of the President. Films, photographs, and a display of the many conspiracy books about the assassination are presented.

El Paso

Chamizal National Memorial Museum
800 South San Marcial
El Paso, TX 79944
Tel. 915-541-7780 or 915-541-7880

Established in 1973, the site commemorates the settlement of boundary disputes between the United States and Mexico. There is an exhibit that summarizes the history of the boundary between the two countries.

Fort Bliss Replica Museum
U.S. Army Air Defense Center
Fort Bliss, TX 79916
Tel. 915-568-2804 or 915-568-4518

Four adobe buildings contain artifacts related to the history of the U.S. Army in the El Paso area.

Hueco Tanks State Park
Rural Route 3, Box 1
El Paso, TX 79935
Tel. 915-857-1135

Rock formations that stored precious water in natural reservoirs, or "tanks," made this area a stopping place for travelers from the time of prehistoric Indians to the 1849 gold rush to California. Indian pictographs as well as the initials of the gold seekers are still visible on the rock walls.

Magoffin Home State Historic Site
1120 Magoffin Avenue
El Paso, TX 79901
Tel. 915-533-5147

James Magoffin settled in the El Paso area in 1849 and his son, Joseph, built this adobe house in 1875. In the 1880s the home was covered with plaster and scored to look like masonry. It is filled with original furnishings and remains in the hands of Magoffin's descendants.

Ysleta del Sur Pueblo Museum
119 South Old Pueblo Road
El Paso, TX 79907
Tel. 915-859-3916

This site represents the oldest continued settlement in the state. The museum tells the story of the Tigua Indians of Texas. Nearby are the Ysleta Mission of 1682 and the Tigua Indian Reservation.

Fort Davis

Fort Davis National Historic Site
State Highway 17
Fort Davis, TX 79734
Tel. 915-426-3225

Established in 1854 as a part of the defense of the road from El Paso to San Antonio, the fort remained in use until 1891. It is now partly restored and features living history demonstrations as well as displays of artifacts.

Fort Worth

Amon Carter Museum of Western Art
3501 Camp Bowie Boulevard
Fort Worth, TX 76107
Tel. 817-738-1933

Opened in 1961, the museum holds one of the finest collections of western art and photographs in the United States. The collection includes works by such prominent artists as Frederic Remington, Charles M. Russell, and Georgia O'Keeffe.

Cattleman's Museum
1301 West Seventh
Fort Worth, TX 76102
Tel. 817-332-7064

Located in the same building as the Texas and Southwestern Cattle Raisers Foundation, this museum reinforces Fort Worth's image as the town where the West begins, with photographs and displays of cowboy equipment. Videos about the history of ranches in Texas are also shown.

Log Cabin Village
University Drive at Log Cabin Village Lane
Fort Worth, TX 76109
Tel. 817-926-5881

Seven authentic log cabins have been moved to the site and restored. Included is a good example of a dogtrot house.

Fritch

Alibates Flint Quarries and Texas Panhandle Pueblo Culture National Monument
U.S. 136
Fritch, TX 79036
Tel. 806-857-3151

Indians over much of the Southwest used flint from these quarries to make a variety of tools—knives, chisels, drills, scrapers, and arrowheads. The site can be seen only on a guided tour limited to 20 people.

Galveston

Ashton Villa
2328 Broadway
Galveston, TX 77553
Tel. 409-762-3933

Built in 1859, this Italianate-style mansion survived the Civil War, the 1900 hurricane, and the threat of demolition to become one of the leading examples of historic preservation in Texas.

Bishop's Palace
1402 Broadway
Galveston, TX 77553
Tel. 409-762-2475

Originally designed by architect Nicholas J. Clayton for Walter Gresham, a wealthy attorney, this turreted Victorian mansion later was the residence of the bishop of Galveston until 1950. The American Institute of Architects named the Bishop's Palace as one of the 100 outstanding buildings in the United States in 1956.

Moody Mansion and Museum
2618 Broadway
Galveston, TX 77550
Tel. 409-762-7668

W. L. Moody, Jr., was one of Galveston's most successful businessmen. His home, a mansion built in 1895, is an example of turn-of-the-century splendor in both furnishings and art.

Samuel May Williams House
3601 Avenue P
Galveston, TX 77553
Tel. 409-765-7834

Samuel May Williams, an early resident of Galveston, had his home prefabricated in Maine and shipped to the island. It has been well restored and equipped with videos that tell about Williams and the history of early Texas.

The Strand
2000-2500 Strand Street
Galveston, TX 77553
Tel. 409-765-7834

Because of its 19th-century commercial buildings, this ten-block area has been designated a National Historic Landmark. Many of the iron-front buildings have been restored and put into use as shops and restaurants. The area is used for Mardi Gras and "Dickens' Evening on the Strand" celebrations.

Elissa
Pier 22
Galveston, TX 77553
Tel. 409-763-0027

Near the Strand is the home port of the *Elissa*, a restored, three-masted "tall ship" built in 1877. It is the only square-rigged ship on the Gulf of Mexico, and volunteers from around South Texas maintain the vessel in working order.

Goliad

Presidio La Bahia Museum
U.S. 183
Goliad, TX 77963
Tel. 512-645-3752

This was the site of the execution of Colonel James Fannin and his men during the Texas Revolution. The presidio and church have been restored with displays of various historic figures who lived in the area. The Mission Espiritu Santo, established at the same time in 1754, is 1.5 miles away.

Houston

Lyndon B. Johnson Space Center
I-45 on NASA Road 1
Houston, TX 77058
Tel. 713-483-4321 or 713-483-4241

At the visitor center there are displays of moon rocks, spacecraft, and historic space equipment. NASA videos are shown regularly. It is from this mission control center that all spaceflights are directed.

San Jacinto Battleground
State Highway 225
Houston, TX 77571
Tel. 713-479-2421

At the base of the San Jacinto Monument is a museum about the history of the Republic of Texas. The observation floor at the top provides a view of the battlefield, the Houston Ship Channel, and the battleship *Texas,* a vessel that fought in both world wars.

Kingsville

John E. Conner Museum
820 West Santa Gertrudis
Texas A&I University
Kingsville, TX 78363
Tel. 512-595-2819

The emphasis of this museum is on Spanish, Mexican, and Texan ranching along with the history of the King Ranch, one of the largest in the world. Tours of the nearby King Ranch can also be arranged.

Livingston

Alabama-Coushatta Indian Reservation
Route 3, P.O. Box 640
Livingston, TX 77351
Tel. 409-563-4391

The land for this reservation was requested by Sam Houston in 1854, and the reservation has been kept since that time. There is a museum that displays the history of the tribes and an active summer schedule, including a "pow-wow" in June.

Lubbock

Ranching Heritage Center
Texas Tech University
Fourth Street and Indiana Avenue
Lubbock, TX 79409
Tel. 806-742-2498

Part of a larger museum complex, the Ranching Heritage Center has collected and reconstructed a series of authentic West Texas buildings including a dugout, various frame ranch houses, a barn, schools, and a train depot. It is an outstanding collection.

Midland

Permian Basin Petroleum Museum
I-20 at State Highway 349
Midland, TX 79701
Tel. 915-683-4403

This museum, dedicated to the history of the oil industry, contains 60,000 items. Of particular interest is the display of various drilling rigs on the ground behind the main building.

Nacogdoches

Stone Fort Museum
Stephen F. Austin State University
Clark Drive and Griffith Boulevard
Nacogdoches, TX 75962
Tel. 409-569-2408

This fort was moved to its present site in 1936 from the town square, where it had existed since 1799. It contains materials relating to the history of East Texas to 1900.

Paint Rock

Paint Rock Excursions
Box 186
Paint Rock, TX 76866
Tel. 915-732-4376 or 915-732-4418

Indian pictographs, 200 to 500 years old, are painted on a rock bluff of the Concho River. The site is on private land and a tour must be arranged.

Rockport

Aransas National Wildlife Refuge
Rockport, TX
Tel. 512-286-3559

Established in 1937 and run by the U.S. Fish and Wildlife Service, these 100,000 acres of marshland are the last refuge of the endangered whooping crane. The area is also home to some 300 other birds. Sight-seeing from observation towers, trails, and cruise boats is best during the winter months.

San Angelo

Fort Concho National Historic Landmark

716 Burgess Street
San Angelo, TX 76903
Tel. 915-655-2121

Twenty-three buildings of the military post have been restored or reconstructed, including barracks, officers' quarters, chapel, headquarters, hospital, and schoolhouse. It was an active post from 1867 to 1889, and the restoration provides a rich view of military life on the Texas frontier.

San Antonio

The Alamo

Alamo Plaza
San Antonio, TX 78299
Tel. 512-225-3853

Maintained by the Daughters of the Republic of Texas, the Alamo is the best-known historic site of the Texas Revolution. Here, the Mexican dictator Santa Anna in 1836 defeated the stubborn Texan defenders, led by William Travis, James Bowie, and Davy Crockett. The museum and grounds portray the battle scene and the history of the revolution.

Institute of Texan Cultures of the University of Texas

HemisFair Plaza
801 South Bowie Street
San Antonio, TX 78205
Tel. 512-226-7651

For a general overview of Texas history, this is the place to go. Exhibits are arranged by the more than 30 ethnic groups that form the population of Texas. The institute has published a series of booklets about each ethnic group and maintains the largest photographic collection about Texas history in the state. A trip to the observation deck of the HemisFair Tower next door gives a panoramic view of San Antonio.

La Villita National Register Historic District

Bolivar Hall, La Villita
San Antonio, TX 78205
Tel. 512-224-6163

This Spanish-Mexican living and shopping area was restored by the Works Progress Administration in the 1930s. Bolivar Hall presents artifacts, maps, and photographs of urban changes. The River Walk, also a depression-era project, borders the La Villita area.

San Antonio Missions National Historical Park

Mission Concepcion
807 Mission Road
San Antonio, TX 78214
Tel. 512-532-3158

There are four Spanish missions, not counting the Alamo, located along the San Antonio River included in the historical park established in 1978. Mission Concepcion is located in the downtown area.

Spanish Governor's Palace

105 Military Plaza
San Antonio, TX 78205
Tel. 512-224-0601

Built between 1722 and 1749, this adobe structure served as a seat of Spanish government in Texas. After 1822 the building was used for various purposes, including a barroom and a schoolhouse. In 1929 the city of San Antonio purchased and restored the building.

Steves Homestead

509 King William Street
San Antonio, TX 78204
Tel. 512-225-5924

This three-story home is a prime example of the mansions that were constructed in the late 19th century in the King William district.

Witte Memorial Museum

1801 Broadway
San Antonio, TX 78209
Tel. 512-226-5544

Dedicated to history and natural history, the Witte has dioramas of birds and wildlife of the region plus a collection of art pertaining to Texas.

Stonewall

Lyndon B. Johnson State Historical Park

U.S. 290
Stonewall, TX 78671
Tel. 512-644-2252

The visitor center provides information about President Johnson's youth, and bus tours by the National Park Service take visitors to the LBJ ranch located across the Pedernales River. The National Park Service also maintains Johnson's childhood home in nearby Johnson City.

Waco

Texas Ranger Hall of Fame and Museum

I-35 and Brazos River
Waco, TX 76703
Tel. 817-754-1433

The Hall of Fame presents 150 years of Texas Ranger history, along with displays of guns and other equipment. Nearby is the Waco suspension bridge, built in 1870 using the same technology that was later used in the Brooklyn Bridge in New York.

Washington

Washington-on-the-Brazos State Historical Park

Washington, TX 77880
Tel. 409-878-2461

Independence Hall, Anson Jones Home, and the Star of the Republic Museum all honor the independence of Texas declared in 1836. Anson Jones was the last president of the republic, and Independence Hall is the building where the Declaration of Independence from Mexico was signed. The museum emphasizes the history of the republic and the role of Washington-on-the-Brazos in Texas history.

Further Reading

General Research and Reference Guides to Texas

Branda, Eldon S., ed. *The Handbook of Texas*. Vol. 3. Austin: Texas State Historical Association, 1976.

Cummins, Light T., and Alvin R. Bailey, Jr., eds. *A Guide to the History of Texas*. Westport, Conn.: Greenwood, 1988.

Immroth, Barbara F. *Texas in Children's Books: An Annotated Bibliography*. Hamden, Conn.: Library Professional Publications, 1986.

Jenkins, John H. *Basic Texas Books*. Austin: Jenkins, 1983.

Stevens, A. Ray, and William M. Holmes. *Historical Atlas of Texas*. Norman: University of Oklahoma Press, 1989.

Texas Almanac and State Industrial Guide. Dallas: Dallas Morning News, biennial.

Tyler, Paula E., and Ron Tyler. *Texas Museums: A Guidebook*. Austin: University of Texas Press, 1983.

Webb, Walter Prescott, ed. *The Handbook of Texas*. 2 vols. Austin: Texas State Historical Association, 1952.

General Histories of Texas

Bones, Jim. *Texas: Images of the Landscape*. Englewood, Colo.: Westcliffe, 1986.

Calvert, Robert A., and Arnoldo De Leon. *The History of Texas*. Arlington Heights, Ill.: Harlan Davidson, 1990.

Casey, Betty. *Dance Across Texas*. Austin: University of Texas Press, 1985.

Doughty, Robin W. *Wildlife and Man in Texas: Environmental Change and Conservation*. College Station: Texas A&M University Press, 1983.

Fehrenbach, T. R. *Lone Star: A History of Texas and Texans*. New York: Macmillan, 1968.

Fehrenbach, T. R., and Bill Ellzey. *Texas: A Salute from Above*. San Antonio: Texas Books, 1985.

Frantz, Joe B. *Texas: A Bicentennial History*. New York: Norton, 1976.

Hendricks, Patricia D., and Becky Duval Reese. *A Century of Sculpture in Texas, 1889–1989*. Austin: University of Texas Press, 1989.

Institute of Texan Cultures of the University of Texas at San Antonio has published the following booklets:

Afro-American Texans (1980), *Belgian Texans* (1980), *Chinese Texans* (1978), *Czech Texans* (1980), *French Texans* (1980), *German Texans* (1970), *Greek Texans* (1974), *Indian Texans* (1979), *Italian Texans* (1980), *Jewish Texans* (1980), *Mexican Texans* (1975), *Norwegian Texans* (1980), *Polish Texans* (1979), *Spanish Texans* (1972), *Swiss Texans* (1977), *Syrian and Lebanese Texans* (1974).

Institute of Texan Cultures. *Ethnic Cuisine in Texas*. San Antonio: Institute of Texan Cultures of the University of Texas at San Antonio, 1977.

Jordan, Terry G. *Texas Graveyards: A Cultural Legacy*. Austin: University of Texas Press, 1982.

McComb, David G. *Texas: A Modern History*. Austin: University of Texas Press, 1989.

Meinig, D. W. *Imperial Texas: An Interpretive Essay in Cultural Geography*. Austin: University of Texas Press, 1969.

Monejano, David. *Anglos and Mexicans in the Making of Texas, 1836–1986*. Austin: University of Texas Press, 1987.

Nevin, David, and the editors of Time-Life Books. *The Texans*. New York: Time-Life Books, 1975.

Ratcliffe, Sam DeShong. *Painting Texas History to 1900*. Austin: University of Texas Press, 1993.

Richardson, Rupert N., et al. *Texas: The Lone Star State*. Englewood Cliffs, N.J.: Prentice-Hall, 1988.

Steinfeldt, Cecilia. *Art for History's Sake*. Austin: Texas State Historical Association, 1993.

Webb, Walter Prescott. *The Great Plains*. New York: Grosset & Dunlap, 1931.

Willoughby, Larry. *Texas Rhythm, Texas Rhyme: a Pictorial History of Texas Music*. Austin: Texas Monthly Press, 1984.

Periodicals About Texas

Insight. A quarterly newsletter for elementary and secondary teachers of history published by the Texas State Historical Association.

These University of Texas students, members of the "Saturday Night Conversation Club," are shown here at their boarding-house around 1900.

Southwestern Historical Quarterly. The professional journal of the Texas State Historical Association.

Texas Historian. This journal of Texas history, sponsored by the Texas State Historical Association, has been written by and for young people since 1940.

Texas Journal of Ideas, History, and Culture. Published by the Texas Committee for the Humanities.

Early Texas

Bedichek, Roy. *Karankaway Country*. Austin: University of Texas Press, 1958.

Bomar, George W. *Texas Weather*. Austin: University of Texas Press, 1983.

Felton, Harold W. *Pecos Bill, Texas Cowpuncher*. New York: Knopf, 1949.

Jenkins, John Holland. *Recollections of Early Texas*. Edited by John Holmes Jenkins III. Austin: University of Texas Press, 1958.

Jordan, Terry G., et al. *Texas: A Geography*. Boulder, Colo.: Westview Press, 1984.

Newcomb, W. W., Jr. *The Indians of Texas*. Austin: University of Texas Press, 1961.

Olmsted, Frederick Law. *A Journey through Texas*. 1857. Reprint. Austin: University of Texas Press, 1978.

Sibley, Marilyn McAdams. *Travelers in Texas, 1761–1860*. Austin: University of Texas Press, 1967.

Smith, Larry L., and Robin W. Doughty. *The Amazing Armadillo*. Austin: University of Texas Press, 1984.

Spanish Texas

Chipman, Donald E. *Spanish Texas, 1519–1821*. Austin: University of Texas Press, 1992.

Covey, Cyclone. *Cabeza de Vaca's Adventures in the Unknown Interior of America*. New York: Collier, 1961.

De Leon, Arnoldo. *They Called Them Greasers*. Austin: University of Texas Press, 1983.

Dobie, J. Frank. *Coronado's Children: Tales of Lost Mines and Buried Treasures of the Southwest*. Dallas: Southwest Press, 1930.

Downs, Fane. "'Tryels and Trubbles': Women in Early Nineteenth-Century

Texas." *Southwestern Historical Quarterly* 90 (July 1986): 33–56.

Ford, John Salmon "Rip." *Rip Ford's Texas*. Edited by Stephen B. Oates. Austin: University of Texas Press, 1963.

Horgan, Paul. *Great River: The Rio Grande in North American History*. New York: Rinehart, 1954.

Jackson, Jack. *Los Mestenos: Spanish Ranching in Texas, 1721–1821*. College Station: Texas A&M University Press, 1986.

John, Elizabeth A. H. *Storms Brewed in Other Men's Worlds*. College Station: Texas A&M University Press, 1975.

Smithwick, Noah. *The Evolution of a State*. Compiled by Nanna Smithwick Donaldson. 1900. New ed. Austin: University of Texas Press, 1983.

Sonnichsen, Charles L. *Pass of the North: Four Centuries on the Rio Grande*. 2 vols. El Paso: Texas Western Press, 1968–1980.

Weber, David J. *The Mexican Frontier, 1821–1846: The American Southwest under Mexico*. Albuquerque: University of New Mexico Press, 1982.

Weddle, Robert S. *The Spanish Sea: The Gulf of Mexico in North American Discovery, 1500–1685*. College Station: Texas A&M University Press, 1985.

Weddle, Robert S. *Wilderness Manhunt: The Spanish Search for La Salle*. Austin: University of Texas Press, 1973.

The Texas Republic

Barker, Eugene C. *The Life of Stephen F. Austin*. Austin: University of Texas Press, 1926.

Barr, Alwyn. *Black Texans: A History of Negroes in Texas, 1528–1971*. Austin: Jenkins, 1973.

Clarke, Mary Whatley. *Chief Bowles and the Texas Cherokees*. Norman: University of Oklahoma Press, 1971.

Exley, Jo Ella Powell, ed. *Texas Tears and Texas Sunshine: Voices of Frontier Women*. College Station: Texas A&M University Press, 1985.

Friend, Llerena. *Sam Houston: The Great Designer*. Austin: University of Texas Press, 1954.

Hill, Jim Dan. *The Texas Navy*. Austin: State House Press, 1987.

Hogan, William Ransom. *The Texas Republic, a Social and Economic History*. Norman: University of Oklahoma Press, 1946.

Hollon, W. Eugene. *William Bollaert's Texas*. Norman: University of Oklahoma Press, 1956.

Pohl, James W. *The Battle of San Jacinto*. Austin: Texas State Historical Association, 1989.

Siegel, Stanley. *A Political History of the Texas Republic, 1836–1845*. Austin: University of Texas Press, 1956.

Silverthorne, Elizabeth. *Plantation Life in Texas*. College Station: Texas A&M University Press, 1986.

Simpson, Harold B. *Hood's Texas Brigade*. Waco: Texian Press, 1970.

Wheeler, Kenneth W. *To Wear a City's Crown: The Beginnings of Urban Growth in Texas, 1836–1865*. Cambridge: Harvard University Press, 1968.

Woolfolk, George R. *The Free Negro in Texas, 1800–1860*. Ann Arbor, Mich.: University Microfilms, 1976.

Wooster, Ralph A., and Robert Wooster. "'Rarin' for a Fight': Texans in the Confederate Army." *Southwestern Historical Quarterly* 84 (April 1981): 387–426.

Frontier Life

Barnett, Douglas E. "Angora Goats in Texas: Agricultural Innovation of the Edwards Plateau, 1858–1900." *Southwestern Historical Quarterly* 90 (April 1987): 347–72.

Blue, Teddy (E. C. Abbott). *We Pointed Them North*. Norman: University of Oklahoma Press, 1939, 1954.

Carlson, Paul H. *Texas Woollybacks: The Texas Sheep and Goat Industry*. College Station: Texas A&M University Press, 1982.

Crawford, Ann Fears, and Crystal S. Ragsdale. *Women in Texas*. Austin: Eakin, 1982.

Dobie, J. Frank. *The Longhorns*. Austin: University of Texas Press, 1985.

Frantz, Joe B., and Julian E. Choate. *The American Cowboy: The Myth and the Reality*. Norman: University of Oklahoma Press, 1955.

Graves, Lawrence L., et al. *History of Lubbock*. Lubbock: West Texas Museum Association, 1962.

Haley, J. Evetts. *Charles Goodnight, Cowman & Plainsman*. Boston: Houghton Mifflin, 1936.

Hollon, W. Eugene. *Beyond the Cross Timbers: The Travels of Randolph B. Marcy, 1812–1887*. Norman: University of Oklahoma Press, 1955.

Knight, Oliver, with Cissy S. Lale. *Fort Worth: Outpost on the Trinity*. Fort Worth: Texas Christian Press, 1990.

Lea, Tom. *The King Ranch*. 2 vols. Boston: Little, Brown, 1957.

Siringo, Charles A. *A Texas Cowboy: or, Fifteen Years on the Hurricane Deck of a Spanish Pony, Taken from Real Life*. Lincoln: University of Nebraska Press, 1979.

Timmons, W. H. *El Paso: A Borderlands History*. El Paso: University of Texas at El Paso, 1990.

Wallace, Ernest. *Ranald S. Mackenzie on the Texas Frontier*. Lubbock: West Texas Museum Association, 1964.

Webb, Walter Prescott. *The Texas Rangers: A Century of Frontier Defense*. Boston: Houghton Mifflin, 1935.

Yasbley, Suzanne. *Texas Quilts, Texas Women*. College Station: Texas A&M University Press, 1984.

The Growth of Modern Texas

Alexander, Charles C. *Crusade for Conformity: The Ku Klux Klan in Texas, 1920–1930*. Houston: Texas Gulf Coast Historical Association, 1962.

Brown, Norman D. *Hood, Bonnet, and Little Brown Jug: Texas Politics, 1921–1928*. College Station: Texas A&M University Press, 1984.

Bryant, Keith L., Jr. *Arthur Stillwell: Promoter with a Hunch*. Nashville: Vanderbilt University Press, 1971.

Clark, James A., and Michael Halbouty. *Spindletop*. New York: Random House, 1952.

Cotner, Robert. *James Stephen Hogg*. Austin: University of Texas Press, 1951.

Cutrer, Emily. *The Art of the Woman: The Life and Work of Elisabet Ney*. Lincoln: University of Nebraska Press, 1988.

Dobie, Bertha McKee, et al. *Growing Up in Texas*. Austin: Encino, 1972.

Frost, H. Gordon, and John H. Jenkins. *I'm Frank Hamer: The Life of a Texas Peace Officer*. Austin: Jenkins, 1968.

Graham, Don. *No Name on the Bullet: A Biography of Audie Murphy*. New York: Viking, 1989.

McComb, David G. *Galveston: A History*. Austin: University of Texas Press, 1986.

McComb, David G. *Houston: A History*. Austin: University of Texas Press, 1981.

Murphy, Audie. *To Hell and Back*. Blue Ridge Summit, Pa.: Tab, 1988.

Olien, Roger M., and Diana Davids Olien. *Life in the Oil Fields*. Austin: Texas Monthly Press, 1986.

O'Neal, Bill. *The Texas League, 1888–1987: A Century of Baseball*. Austin: Eakin, 1987.

Paredes, Americo. *With His Pistol in His Hand*. Austin: University of Texas Press, 1958.

Payne, Darwin. *Dallas: An Illustrated History*. Woodland Hills, Calif.: Windsor, 1982.

Roberts, Randy. *Papa Jack: Jack Johnson and the Era of White Hopes*. New York: Free Press, 1983.

Timmons, Bascom. *Jesse Jones*. New York: Holt, Rinehart & Winston, 1956.

Tinkle, Lon. *Mr. D.: A Biography of Everette Lee DeGolyer*. Boston: Little, Brown, 1970.

Whisenhunt, Donald W. *The Depression in Texas: The Hoover Years*. New York: Garland, 1983.

Texas Today

Bainbridge, John. *Super-Americans*. Garden City, N.Y.: Doubleday, 1961.

Bissinger, H. G. *Friday Night Lights: A Town, a Team, and a Dream*. New York: Addison-Wesley, 1990.

Chasins, Abram, and Villa Stiles. *The Van Cliburn Legend*. Garden City, N.Y.: Doubleday, 1959.

Conkin, Paul. *Big Daddy from the Pedernales: Lyndon Baines Johnson*. Boston: Twayne, 1986.

Dallek, Robert. *Lone Star Rising: Lyndon Johnson and His Times, 1908–1960*. New York: Oxford University Press, 1991.

Dugger, Ronnie, ed. *Three Men in Texas*. Austin: University of Texas Press, 1967.

Greene, A. C. *Dallas, USA*. Austin: Texas Monthly Press, 1984.

Johnson, Lady Bird. *White House Diary*. New York: Holt, Rinehart & Winston, 1970.

Jordan, Barbara, and Shelby Hearon. *Barbara Jordan: A Self Portrait*. Garden City, N.Y.: Doubleday, 1979.

Lasher, Patricia. *Texas Women: Interviews & Images*. Austin: Shoal Creek, 1980.

O'Connor, Robert F., ed. *Texas Myths*. College Station: Texas A&M University Press, 1986.

Pilkington, William T. *Imagining Texas: The Literature of the Lone Star State*. Boston: American Press, 1981.

Williamson, Nancy P. *Whatta-gal! The Babe Didrikson Story*. Boston: Little, Brown, 1977.

Winningham, Geoff, and Al Reinert. *Rites of Fall: High School Football in Texas*. Austin: University of Texas Press, 1979.

References to illustrations are indicated by page numbers in *italics*.

Nation, Carrie, 103
Navarro, José, 45
Navy, Texas, *45, 46*
Neal, Margie, 98
Neches, Battle of, 42
Nelson, Willie, *110*
Newman, Barnett, 123
Ney, Elisabet, *89*
Niza, Father Marcos de, 22
Nocona, Peta, 56

Oil industry, 90-96, 128-29
Olivares, Father Antonio de, 38
O'Reilly, Tex, 17
Ortiz de Parilla, Col. Diego, 25
Oswald, Lee Harvey, 113

Paleo-Indian skeletons, 7-9
Palmito Ranch, Battle of, 60
Parker, Cynthia Ann, 44, *54,* 55-56
Parker, Quanah, 56, 66-67
Pease, Elisha M., 62
Pease River, Battle of, 55
Pecos Bill, 17
Perfecto de Cós, Gen. Martín, 33, 37
Perot, H. Ross, 118, *119*
Pershing, Gen. John F. "Blackjack,"
 100
Philosophical Society of Texas, 88
Piñeda, Alonso Alvarez de, 22
Political Association of Spanish-
 Speaking Organizations, 117
Politics, 117-22
Polk, James K., 47-48
Pollution, 126-27
Ponton, Andrew, 32
Population
 of cities, 82-83, 127
 of Texas, 28, 49, 65, 129
Post, Charles William, *90*
Potter, Alexander, 81
Prohibition, 99, 102-3

Rabb, Mary, 36
Racial segregation, 85-86, 102, 114-15
Railroads, 55, 65, 75-77, *78, 79,* 83
Range wars, 74
Rattlesnakes, 18, 70
Raza Unida, La, 117
Reconstruction period, 59, 61-63
Republican party, 62-63, 119
Revolution (Texas), 33-39
Richards, Ann W., 119, *120*
Richardson, Sid, 69
Rivers, 13
Robinson, James, 33
Rock art, Indian, *14*
Rocky Mountains, 12
Rodeo, *112*
Roosevelt, Franklin D., *105,* 121
Rothko, Mark, 123
Ruby, George T., 62

Ruby, Jack, 113
Rusk, Thomas J., 47, *48*

Saint-Denis, Louis Juchereau de, 26
Saligny, Alphonse Dubois de, 43
San Antonio de Valero Mission. *See*
 Alamo Mission
San Antonio, Texas, 15, 27-28, 50, *55,*
 79, *82,* 83, *115, 116*
San Fernando de Bexar, *28*
San Jacinto, Battle of, 36-37, *39*
San José Mission, *26*
San Saba Mission, 25
Santa Anna, Antonio López de, 32-39,
 41, 46, 49
Santa Fe expedition of 1841, 45
Schreiner, Charles, 71
Scott, Gen. Winfield, 48, *49*
Secession movement, 56-57
Segregation, racial. *See* Racial
 segregation
Sewage disposal systems, 81
Sharp, Walter B., 93
Sheep industry, 71, *72*
Sheridan, Gen. Philip, 17, 62
Sherman, Gen. William Tecumseh,
 65-67
Shivers, Allen, 115
Slavery, 27, 29, 30, 32, 53-54, 56, 62
Smith, Henry, 33
Smithwick, Noah, 30, 44, 54
Snakes, poisonous, 18
Spanish explorations, 21-24
Spanish missionaries, *20,* 24-28
Spindletop oil well, 92
Sports, 85-87, 112, 124-26
Stallings, James, 73
Statehood for Texas, 41, 47
Sterling, Ross S., 95
Streetcars, *82*
Sweatt, Herman Marion, *114*
Sweatt v. *Painter, 114*

Taychas Indians, 9
Taylor, Gen. Zachary, 48-49
Telegraph, 79
Telephone, 79
Terraqueous machine, *50*
Texas Historical Association, 89
Texas Library Association, 80, 88
Texas Rangers, 42, 45, 74, *75,* 94-95,
 109-10, 115
Theater, 111
Thomas, Albert, 122
Throckmorton, James W., *61,* 62
Tigua Indians, 12, 56, 68
Tonkawa Indians, 11-12, 25
Tornadoes, 16-17
Tower, John, 119
Transportation, 50, 55, 81-82, 100, 126
Travis, William B., 32, 33, 34
Trist, Nicholas, 49

Ugartecha, Col. Domingo de, 32-33
Urrea, Gen. José, 33-34

Velasco, Treaty of, 39
Villa, Pancho, *100,* 101
Voting rights
 for African Americans, 62, 121
 for women, 63, 103, *104*

Waco, Texas, 7, 15, 17, 89, *91*
Waggoneer, William T., 94
Walker, William Aiken, *26*
Wallace, Maj. H. A., 59
Wallace, William A. A. "Big Foot," 47
Water resources, 13, 51, 72, 81
 irrigation projects, 27, *29*
 and windmills, *73*
Weapons, *11,* 25, *37*
Weather conditions, 16-18
Webb, Walter Prescott, 109, *110*
White, James Taylor, 68
White, Mark, 118, 119
Wichita Indians, 9, 23, 25
Wilderness conservation, 99-100
Wildlife resources, 15, 18-19
Williams, Lizzie, 69-70
Williamson, Charles N., 97
Willingham, Cape, 71
Wills, Bob, 110
Wilson, Woodrow, 100
World War I, 101, *102,* 103
World War II, 105-7

Yellow fever epidemics, 59-62
Young, Wayne, 7

Zaharias, Babe Didrikson, 126

Picture Credits

About the Author

David G. McComb is a displaced Texan currently living in Colorado, where he is professor of history at Colorado State University. He grew up in Houston and graduated from Southern Methodist University. He holds an M.B.A. from Stanford University, an M.A. from Rice University, and a Ph.D. from the University of Texas at Austin. Professor McComb is the author of *Texas: A Modern History, Houston: The Bayou City* (winner of the Tullis Prize of the Texas State Historical Association), *Galveston: A History* (winner of the Texas State Historical Commission Book Award), and *Colorado: A History of the Centennial State*. He was a special research associate of the University of Texas Oral History Project on Lyndon B. Johnson and is a fellow of the Texas State Historical Association.